Praise for *Breaking Addiction*

"In *Breaking Addiction*, Dr. Dodes looks beneath the surface behaviors of addiction to root it out at its source. Without denying the difficulty of the terrain, Dodes's program offers a clear-eyed, coherent approach. This groundbreaking work should become the 'go-to' handbook for anyone suffering with addiction. Its easy-to-read style takes sophisticated ideas and turns them into memorable examples. I highly recommend it."

—Edward Hallowell, MD, author of *Answers to Distraction* and *Superparenting for ADD*

"Lance Dodes has written a brave, wise, and humane book. *Breaking Addiction* empowers addicts to take responsibility and reclaim their own agency so that they can overcome their addictions. His approach runs directly counter to the paralyzing, but standard, message of 'powerlessness'—a message that reinforces the sense of helplessness that is at the root of addicts' life predicaments! Many psychiatrists recognize that this is where we must head, but Dr. Dodes is one with the guts to shine a beacon in the right direction."

—Stanton Peele, PhD, author of *7 Tools to Beat Addiction* and *The Life Process Program of Treatment*

"Dr. Dodes combines his insight as one of our most experienced clinicians with many compelling tales of recovery among patients he has successfully treated. You could not ask for a more thoughtful and readable book on ways to deal with the complex and disheartening problem of addiction."

—Marc Galanter, MD, professor of psychiatry, director, division of alcoholism and drug abuse, NYU School of Medicine

"*Breaking Addiction* is destined to become a self-help classic for understanding repetitive, excessive, and self-destructive behavior patterns. Like *The Heart of Addiction*, this book is revolutionary—it provides a map for both understanding and changing seemingly intractable patterns of behavior. Dr. Dodes transforms helplessness into helpfulness; he changes the narrow view of addiction as a brain disease into a rich and useful mindful view of addiction. With case illustrations and cutting-edge insight, this book changes how we understand and react to that panoply of issues that surround addiction. Not only a self-help guide, *Breaking Addiction* belongs on the shelf of every treatment professional because it will improve professional treatment strategies and tactics."

—Howard J. Shaffer, PhD, CAS, associate professor,
Harvard Medical School, director, division on addictions,
the Cambridge Health Alliance (a Harvard Medical School
teaching affiliate)

"*Breaking Addiction* explains why people turn to addictions despite the high price they exact. Through vivid examples and keen insights Dodes shows why addictions are so compelling and advances fresh and practical pathways to understand and deal with addictive behavior. By improving our understanding of the very nature of addiction, Dodes helps people with addictive problems overcome stigma and regain their dignity."

—Edward J. Khantzian, MD, clinical professor of psychiatry,
Harvard Medical School, associate chief emeritus of psychiatry,
Tewksbury Hospital

About the Author

LANCE DODES, MD, a psychiatrist and psychoanalyst, is assistant clinical professor of psychiatry at Harvard Medical School, where he is a member of the Division on Addictions. He has been the director of the substance abuse treatment unit of Harvard's McLean Hospital, director of the alcoholism treatment unit at Spaulding Rehabilitation Hospital (now part of Massachusetts General Hospital), and director of the Boston Center for Problem Gambling, as well as a consultant to other addiction treatment programs. He is the author of the groundbreaking book *The Heart of Addiction*. Dr. Dodes has been honored by the Division on Addictions at Harvard Medical School for Distinguished Contribution to the study and treatment of addictive behavior and has been elected a distinguished fellow of the American Academy of Addiction Psychiatry. His work has been published in many professional journals.

ALSO BY LANCE DODES

——

The Heart of Addiction

BREAKING ADDICTION

A 7-Step Handbook
for Ending Any Addiction

LANCE DODES, MD

HARPER

NEW YORK • LONDON • TORONTO • SYDNEY

HARPER

This book is written as a source of information only. The information contained in this book should by no means be considered a substitute for advice of a qualified medical professional, who should always be consulted before beginning any new health program. All efforts have been made to ensure the accuracy of the information contained in this book as of the date published. The author and the publisher expressly disclaim responsibility for any adverse effects arising from the use or application of the information contained herein.

All cases are composites; persons and situations are based in fact, but names, traits, and circumstances have been changed.

FIRST EDITION

Library of Congress Cataloging-in-Publication Data

Dodes, Lance M.
   Breaking addiction : a 7-step handbook for ending any addiction /
Lance M. Dodes. — 1st ed.
      p. cm.
   ISBN 978-0-06-198739-7 (pbk.)
   1. Substance abuse—Prevention. 2. Substance abuse—Psychological
aspects. 3. Substance abuse—Treatment. I. Title.
   HV4998.D63 2011
   616.86'06—dc22   2010032459

16 17 18   RRD   20 19 18 17 16 15 14 13

For Connie

CONTENTS

BREAKING
ADDICTION

Introduction

It was one o'clock and Ron Golding returned to his desk from lunch to find a manila envelope sitting there, laid on top of the papers he'd been working on. He looked at the outside of the folder. It was from Accounting. "E-mail isn't good enough for them?" he said with annoyance as he opened the envelope. Inside, there was a thick stapled pile of forms with a cover sheet. He glanced at the forms. They were filled with questions and boxes to be checked. He dropped them on his desk and read the cover note. "Dear Ron," it began, "We need to have these filled out by 5 PM and returned, signed. It's for the quarterly report and the legal people say it has to be in their hands today. Sorry! Beth." Now he dropped the letter and picked up the stack of forms again, stared at them, and finally sat down. Turning the pages of forms, he shook his head. "Damn," he said.

"Hey Joey," he called.

Joey was at his own desk only ten feet away. "Yeah?"

"Hey, did you get a pack of crap to fill out for Accounting?"

Joey made a gesture at his own desk. "Yep, I got it."

"Well I can't do it," Ron said. "I've got too much to do."

"I know what you mean."

"No," Ron said, "you don't understand. I mean I really can't do it. Larry is on my back to get a draft to him by tomorrow morning." He leafed through the forms again. "There's at least an hour of work here. And look at it! It's idiotic." He shook his head again. "It's just a damned waste of time. My time, your time, everybody's time."

"I'm with you," Joey said, but he turned back to his computer and seemed done with the exchange.

Ron ran his hand through his hair, and then picked up the phone."Ginny," he said when his wife answered, "I'm going to be late tonight . . . I know, but I have to stay and get this done . . . Probably about seven . . . Just tell the kids we'll make the fort tomorrow . . . I know . . . Yeah, see you then."

He leaned back in his chair. At that moment he knew what he was going to do when he finally got out of there. Ginny didn't like him coming home and drinking, but he sure as hell was going to get a drink tonight. At the bar on the way home. Maybe more than one. He looked down at the pile of forms. Yeah, definitely more than one. He sat forward. Now that he'd decided to go drinking he felt less stressed. Now he could get to work.

———

What is addiction? We are barraged with theories that attempt to answer this question. If you suffer with an addiction or care about someone with an addiction, you may already have found that a lot of people are not able to get well with the usual treatment approaches. This book describes a new way of understanding and managing addiction that I have been writing about in professional journals for the past twenty years, and summarized in a previous book, *The Heart of Addiction* (HarperCollins, 2002).

As the director or psychiatric consultant for four major addiction treatment programs, and as a therapist in private practice for over thirty years, I developed my ideas not by telling people what they should do, but by listening carefully to them to understand the reasons why they had an addiction, why it became so hard to control, and why it overwhelmed them when it did. Over time, I came to see addiction in a new way, one that is very different from older approaches. Indeed, if you are used to those older ideas you may find these new concepts a bit jarring. But since the publication of my first book these ideas and methods have been utilized by therapists and treatment centers and taught in educational programs around the country.

Breaking Addiction is the result of feedback I've received indicating the need for a more hands-on, step-by-step blueprint to make this new approach more accessible—for people suffering with addictions, for those who live with them and care about them, and for those who treat them. This book is also intended to help you if you are unsure whether or not you have an addiction, or if your interest is just to better understand the nature of addiction.

HOW THIS BOOK IS ORGANIZED

In Part One I will summarize how addictions work, continuing the story of Ron (above) to illustrate this. I'll turn, in Part Two of the book, to the individual steps in the mastery of addiction—from the beginning to the end of the process, illustrating each step with case examples. The final chapter of Part Two is entitled "Test Yourself"; it's designed to give you the chance to apply what you've learned to the stories of several people suffering with addiction. Part Three is a guide for family members and loved ones of people with addictions. As you'll see, once you understand how addiction really works, you are in an excellent position to repair relationships and families that have been damaged by addiction. Finally, Part Four specifically addresses professionals who treat addiction, describing ways this new approach can serve as the foundation for professional treatment.

PART I

A New Way to Understand Addiction

Everyone knows that addictive behavior is not good for you. People who suffer with addictions may know this best of all, because they've lived it. But addiction persists. Strange as it may seem, it must serve some purpose. In fact, its purpose must be so great that it is *even more essential* than avoiding the bad consequences of the addiction. It has to be more important than losing marriages, families, friends, jobs, and health. It has to be more important than losing your license to drive or to practice in a field that you care deeply about, more important than the pain of hurting people you love. What could possibly be worth all of that?

In terms of the outside world, the world of careers, family, and success, there is, indeed, nothing worth losing it all. The purpose of addiction must lie in the inside world, where what is at stake are feelings central to emotional survival itself. If this is the case, then nobody would be surprised to find that it overrules even the most important external causes. Let's return to Ron, from the introduction, to see how this works.

RON

When Ron was seven years old he was playing in his room (that he shared with his older brother) when he heard shouting between his parents. This happened a lot. He caught many of the words when they were loud, but most of it meant nothing to him. Something about money, usually. But he felt the familiar sense of torn loyalties and he wished his parents would just stop. The noise ended and a moment later his mother came into the room.

"Ron, I have a headache and I'm going to lie down. Company is coming over and I need you to straighten up the living room. And put the bathroom towels in the laundry, please."

"I'm in the middle of building a Lego castle, Mom."

"I really need you to do this for me now."

"Can I just finish this part? Look, see—I've got the wall all up on this side, and . . ."

"Ronald, I need you to do this right now."

"Can I just show you?"

But his Mom had turned around and was walking up the hall to her room.

After cleaning up, Ron was returning to his room when his father saw him.

"Hey, Ron, come here."

Ron walked over and looked up at his father.

"Listen, I've got to take your brother to his baseball practice so I need you to take out the dog."

"Aw, Dad, I'm in the middle of building a castle."

"Sorry, kid, plans have just been shaken up. Your mother was going to take Ben to practice but now I've got to do it."

"Aw, Dad, do you have to go right now? The castle is standing up and I just need to . . ."

"Talk to your mother about it," his father said, grabbing his keys from the side table before going out back to get Ben.

When Ron was twelve years old his parents' fighting had increased. There was trouble with Ben, who was now a fourteen-year-old giant and rarely listened to either parent, which seemed to Ron to make things that much worse in the home for everyone. Ron had regularly fought with Ben over the years the way brothers do, but now it was worse because there was no fighting. Ben just ignored him. Ron did his best to interest Ben in anything Ron could think of, but capturing his older brother's attention was a lost cause.

Ron's mother seemed to need him even more to help her out, since she spent more and more time in bed. His father had become more tightly strung too. Ron tried hard to keep the peace, but the task was impossible.

Ron was washing dishes for his mother when his father called from the garage.

"Hey, Ron, I need you out here."

"I'm doing the dishes."

"For your mother?"

"Yeah, she's not feeling well."

"Bullshit!" his father said. "When *does* she feel well? Come out here and help me drag this mower out of the corner. It's a mess over here."

"Mom said she needs . . ."

"I don't really give a good goddamn what she needs. Get over here and help me."

Ron dried his hands and went out the back door. He thought about shooting baskets at the outdoor court nearby. Jump shots, driving to the hoop, fooling around with the hook shot he was forever working on. That's what *he* wanted to do.

Twenty years later when Ron got the stapled pile of forms to complete before 5:00 PM, he was furious. Others had gotten the same forms but they weren't nearly as upset. What set off Ron? And what did deciding to have a drink have to do with fixing the problem? Knowing something about him, it's simpler now to figure this out. Ron grew up with some lasting scars. In itself, of course, this doesn't make him unusual. Nobody comes through childhood without at least a few marks and bruises, both physical and emotional. Just from the couple of incidents I described, you can probably make a good guess what these were for Ron. Ron felt unheard. Even though both his mother and father loved him, they were too often preoccupied with their own concerns, including their battles with each other. The fact that his parents loved him enabled him to grow up generally healthy, from an emotional standpoint. But being loved was not enough without also being shown that his parents were deeply interested in the things that were important to him, interested just because they were important to him. Like all children, Ron needed to know that he was a priority in their lives. But it was clear to Ron—though he might not have been able to put it into words as a child—that his parents' priority was their own needs. He was somewhere lower on the list.

And Ron worked hard to comply with their view. He wanted peace, and he wanted to please both his parents, even when they each demanded different things from him. In the end, he adapted by treating himself the way they treated him: he sacrificed his needs for theirs, out of his longing for them and to be heard by them. This got him through the years, but it left a scar. Over and over he had burned with resentment at feeling overlooked, an anger he could not express to the parents he loved. Partly this was because he already felt hopeless about being heard. And he was trying to make peace in the family, not more trouble like his brother was doing. He was trapped. Unheard and helpless to make himself heard. And by trying to give his parents what they expected, he became part of the very system that enveloped him. Quite unintentionally he added to his own sense of helplessness.

So, what happened when Ron got the forms twenty years later? The company needed them by 5:00. They also needed his draft to be prepared by tomorrow. His wife needed him home, and so did his kids. They couldn't all be pleased. It was impossible. Oh and by the way, he thought, did anybody ask what *he* needed? Did anybody think about the bind they were putting him in? In his frustration he thought that when it came down to it, did anybody care, did anybody listen?

Ron was trapped in the way he'd felt helpless his whole life. That was when he thought about drinking.

THE PURPOSE OF ADDICTION

I asked earlier what could be so important that it would lead otherwise sensible, intelligent people to ruin their lives by repeating an addictive behavior. Ron's story illustrates the answer. When he thought of having a drink, he felt better. Importantly, this was not because he had any alcohol in his body; it was enough for him to anticipate having it. To understand why this helped we need only look at the feeling he had at the key moment when he first considered drinking. Once Ron had touched on the idea of stopping by the bar on his way home, he was able to get to work on his forms. He had felt instantly relieved. Why?

The answer is that Ron's decision to drink relieved his feeling of helplessness. He could, entirely in his own control, take an action that would make him feel better. He was the master of his internal life, of his feelings. And he was taking control over not just any helplessness, but the kind that touched on the central emotional problem of his life. Sure, he was still realistically mired in contradictory outside obligations between home and work. But at that key moment what mattered to his very core was reversing this particular sense of helplessness that was now, and had always been, intolerable to him. By God, he might have to work late but he was not going to be a pawn pushed around by the needs of others. Not that day.

This is the purpose of addiction:

Addiction is a behavior intended to reverse a profound, intolerable sense of helplessness. This helplessness is always rooted in something deeply important to the individual.

WHY UNDERSTANDING THE PURPOSE OF ADDICTION MATTERS

- Because it explains why people with addictions are not weaker than people without addictions: people suffering with addictions put up with helplessness just like everyone else as long as it doesn't involve major issues for them. If you have an addiction you know this very well. You are quite able to put up with most day-to-day frustrations without necessarily feeling you need a drink or to place a bet or to eat. Just like everyone else you deal with the ordinary brickbats of life without needing to turn to your addiction. Understanding this—that the purpose of addiction involves managing deeply important feelings—helps to undercut the mistaken idea that people with addictions are weak or fragile. I will return to this point in Step 2.

- Because having an addiction is not the same as being impulsive. This is another common myth. To the contrary, folks with addictions tolerate delay regularly, often even when they are pursuing their addiction. Ron's delay before going out to drink is a common example. (I'll address this important point further in Part Two.)

- Because addressing feelings of helplessness is key to treating addiction. Since the things that set off urges to perform an addictive act are always related in some way to something very important to you, it turns out that if you can figure out this underlying theme you have also figured out something essential about yourself. The issues that provoke an addiction solution are the same as the main emotional troubles you have faced in your life. This might seem a little surprising at first, especially if you've thought about addiction as "separate" from the rest of you or your life. But really it's inevitable since you are only one person. Symptoms such as addictions arise from the same sources as what might make you depressed, or anxious, or have trouble in relationships. And since addictions are linked to who you are, understanding them is worth pursuing even beyond mastering the behavior. Understanding the root of your particular addiction provides an ideal pathway toward understanding yourself altogether.[1]

- Because once we understand the emotional foundation of the addictive drive, it becomes clear that drugs—and their effects on the brain—play a minimal role in addiction. Of course, many addictions involve drugs. And drugs are particularly good for the purposes of addiction, since changing your internal emotional state in a way *you* control is exactly what they

---

[1] Sigmund Freud famously said that dreams are the "royal road to the unconscious" because they provide more direct access to deeper parts of the mind that are not otherwise easily seen. I've found that working to understand addictions can also be a "royal road." Like some dreams, addictions are a kind of shortcut to understanding yourself, a signpost pointing directly to your central problems.

do. They're almost ideal as a (temporary) solution to feeling overwhelmed. Consequently, all kinds of drugs are used addictively (that is, in a compulsive, driven way). But many addictions do not involve drugs at all, and often people can substitute a nondrug compulsive activity such as gambling or cleaning their house, for compulsive use of drugs. This is a good indication that the physical effects of drugs themselves have nothing fundamentally to do with the roots of addiction. I will return to this important point in the next chapter.

Understanding the purpose of addiction is only one part of our mission to understand how addiction works. The next part is just as critical. We all know that when people have the urge to enact their addiction it isn't simply an intellectual decision. There is a huge amount of energy behind addictive acts; there is a powerful *drive* in addiction. We need to know what that drive is.

THE DRIVE BEHIND ADDICTION: WHAT GIVES IT THAT INTENSE FEELING?

Let's return to Ron's story:

Time had passed and now it was 6:15. Ron had finished filling out the accounting forms and finally completed the draft report for his boss. He got up, put on his coat, and headed for the office door thinking about the bar and his first drink. The elevator arrived and he rode it to the basement where he had parked his car. Soon he was driving, but there was traffic—a lot of traffic. Ron was a reverse commuter—he lived in the city and his job was out of town—so rush hour traffic usually favored him both ends of the day. But he had forgotten that whenever he left late he hit the going-into-the-city-for-the-evening traffic. Another thing he had forgotten was that the local baseball team was at home. He saw the line of red taillights bunch up ahead of him and he slowed gradually until he came to a complete stop, surrounded by a few thousand baseball fans on their way to the 7:00 PM start of the game.

Ron had always been a very patient man. But tonight he felt anger building within him. The bar wasn't that far away now, but at this speed, currently zero, it might as well be on Mars. On his left a car tried to move into his lane. Ron slammed on his horn. The car continued to inch over the divider lines. Ron hit the horn again, this time holding it down.

"What the fuck do you think you're trying to do?" he shouted from inside his car. His face was turning red. The other driver seemed oblivious. Ron started to bang his fist on his dashboard, screaming at the other driver. By this point the veins in his neck had become blue ropes. Finally the other driver seemed to notice Ron. He pulled back into his own lane and waved his hand in the universal "sorry, my fault" gesture. Ron resisted the urge to give the other driver the finger, but he continued to breathe hard for another full minute. He noticed that his hands were trembling.

Ron's reaction was rage. But rage at what? He had been in bumper-to-bumper traffic a million times, and had cars try to cut in on him a few thousand times. He had never reacted like this. But this was different. This time he was heading for a drink. Nothing and no one was going to stop him. Nothing was going to get in his way. What he felt wasn't about being cut off in traffic; it was about the rageful intensity of his drive to have a drink.

Ron's reaction was absolutely characteristic of the feeling that drives people toward their addictive acts. In fact, if you think of how rage reveals itself, you will see that it looks remarkably like addiction. In the throes of rage people are overwhelmed with their anger; their rational thinking process and their self-control dissolves. They become unconcerned about the long-term consequences of their actions. Everything in their lives that they normally care about becomes secondary to the expression of the rage. Sounds like addiction, doesn't it? That's not a coincidence, because it is a kind of rage that drives addiction, and this rage gives addiction its characteristic loss of control and seeming irrationality. It is intense rage that leads people with addictions to do things that crush their hopes and plans for the future. Later, of course, they suffer with very genuine regret, as you surely know if you suffer with an addiction yourself. But there is no room for regret when you are in the throes of the rage.

———

This raises the next obvious question. If rage is the drive behind addiction, then what is this rage about? To answer this question we have only to go back to the fact that the function (purpose) of addiction is to reverse a sense of helplessness. Helplessness in anyone normally produces anger, or in the case of extreme helplessness, rage. Think about times when you have been trapped or powerless. Those situations get you fired up emotionally, and they should. All animals react with aggression to being trapped; it's a necessary survival instinct. So, the answer to the question is this:

The drive in addictive behavior is rage at helplessness. It is this particular kind of rage that gives addiction its most conspicuous characteristics of intensity and loss of control.

This fury in addiction is actually quite normal. I sometimes describe it using the analogy of being caught in a cave-in. When you first find yourself trapped in a tight, dark space you might try to stay calm, but that won't last for long. Soon you'll be banging on the rocks, clawing at them to get out. Your hands will be bloody. You might break your wrist in the desperate effort. But that wouldn't matter. At that moment the normal rage in such situations is the dominant force.

It also follows that to say people with addictions are self-destructive is nonsensical. This common myth comes from people looking only at the disastrous results of addictive behavior, rather than what causes it. The person who breaks his wrist when struggling to get out of the cave is hardly self-destructive. The fact is that if you have an addiction you are no more inherently or intentionally self-destructive than anyone else.

The reason addiction works out so badly is not because of the emotional energy driving it, but because this drive arises not just in realistic circumstances like being trapped in a cave, but also in situations that feel overwhelming and confining only to the person suffering with the addiction.

HOW DOES ADDICTION TAKE THE SPECIFIC FORMS IT DOES?

When Ron felt stuck at work he needed to reverse an old sense of helplessness that was revived for him in that situation. But what did alcohol have to do with this? And what does taking other drugs, or compulsively eating, or using the Internet, or spending money, or exercising have to do with the purpose and drive in addiction? What makes addiction take the forms it does?

We can return to Ron to think about this. When he was fuming at his desk at 1:00 PM, his problem was that there were things he had to do and he could see no realistic way out of it. But he had to do *something*. For Ron, that something was drinking alcohol. If he were a compulsive gambler, then his mind would have burned with the thought of going to the casino or buying lottery tickets. The point is that when there is no *direct* action a person feels he or she can take to deal with overwhelming helplessness, he finds a substitute (or a *displaced*) action. This is what makes addiction look the way it does.

Addictions are all substitute (or displaced) actions. They take the place of a more direct response to feelings of helplessness in a particular situation.

In fact, we use these substitute or displaced actions as the labels for addictions themselves. If you compulsively substitute drinking for a direct action, then we say you have alcoholism. If you substitute sex, then we call this a sexual addiction. If you substitute compulsive eating, then we call it a type of eating disorder, and so on. Why individuals find themselves drawn to one displaced action over another is an interesting question. Sometimes it is because that action is personally meaningful. Certain compulsive sexual activities may have a personally important meaning, for example. But often the form of an addiction does not have special meaning, as in most cases of alcoholism. Here, the form of the addiction is a displacement shared by many people who are in other ways vastly different from each other. Their focus on alcohol has more to do with the nearly universal use of alcohol in our society, and sometimes with identification with other important people in their lives who already use alcohol as a solution to emotional distress.

WHY IS THERE A NEED FOR DISPLACEMENT IN ADDICTION?

People perform addictive acts in the face of overwhelming feelings of helplessness because they feel trapped and don't see more direct ways to handle a given situation. Yet in the sorts of scenarios that give rise to addictive thoughts, often there are choices. Looking again at Ron's story, what alternatives did he have? Well, what if he had gone in to see his boss right when he received the forms to complete. He might have said something like, "Look, Larry, I just got this work that Accounting says I have to have back to them today. I can't do it and still get the draft report to you for tomorrow morning. Can you help me out with this? Maybe call Accounting? Or, can I get the report to you by the end of the day tomorrow, instead? My problem with staying late today is that I made a special promise to my kids to do something with them today." What would have happened if Ron did this?

There are a couple of possibilities. It's not a perfect world and maybe Larry would have said, "I'm sorry, but there's nothing I can do. My talking to Accounting won't make any difference, and I absolutely need that report by the morning." This would be the worst-case result. But even here, it's quite possible that Ron would feel a bit less helpless just for having made some effort to deal with his situation. And even with this result he might feel that he had gained something. Maybe he put it in Larry's head that he owed one to Ron because he had taken such a tough line. Next time, perhaps Larry would be more flexible. It is also possible that the worst wouldn't occur. Maybe Larry would have been glad to be flexible. Maybe he would have come up with a compromise, like telling Ron he could present his report in outline form since it was only a draft, anyway.

Besides, going to Larry didn't really exhaust Ron's options. He might have done a quicker, less polished version of the draft on his own. He might have gone home to play with his kids and come in early to work the next morning. He might even have ignored the forms and lived with the complaints from Accounting. The point is that Ron didn't seriously consider any of these possibilities. Why not?

The answer has to do with why displacement is necessary in addiction. Ron didn't consider the practical, direct alternatives because he was already immersed in his old trap. He was already outraged and, at the same time, already feeling he had to contain himself, keep the peace, and please these new "parents" in accounting and his own boss. Without any idea that these issues were distorting his perception of the situation, or that his urge to drink was his solution to this trap, he was overwhelmed.

But when people do understand the way addiction works, they usually can find some more direct action to deal with their helplessness. When they do, they have become the master of their addiction rather than its slave. For Ron, especially knowing his tendency to drink, he would have been focused on finding that more direct solution.

Of course, this is sometimes harder than it might sound. In Ron's case, feeling immersed in the old, central conflicts of his life not only kept him from thinking through his realistic options, but in effect pushed him away from them. Remember, Ron had developed a way to deal with his parents' contradictory demands on him and the tensions between them that were so painful to him as a child. A big part of his solution was to ignore his feelings and keep the peace. Going to his boss to ask for relief from his tasks meant challenging the demands upon him. For Ron, who needed to keep from asking too much and adding to the din around him, that was not an option. Paradoxically, then, in the end Ron was the source of his own helplessness. It was Ron who limited his potential responses at the office just as he had always done.

Limiting oneself is very common in addictions. Ron needed to keep peace, but other people with addictions may limit themselves in other ways. They might worry that acting directly would be inappropriate or immoral, or that acting on what they really feel would make them undesirable. Each person with an addiction is different.

Understanding how your personal issues may limit you from acting directly is often a very important part of resolving an addiction. I will show many examples of people doing just this in later sections.

The fact that people have a role in perpetuating their own suffering is both bad news and good news. The bad news is that it didn't take a realistically major event to set off Ron's addiction. He didn't need to be trapped in a cave-in. Like everyone else with an addiction, in just living ordinary life he was prone to re-experiencing the kind of helplessness to which he had been primed. It was the way he personally experienced events that was the real trigger for him.

The good news, though, is very good. If addiction depended entirely on external events, nobody suffering with an addiction would have much control over it. Since addiction is a symptom, a way to deal with certain overwhelming feelings of helplessness, once you know what the key issues are for you, you are in position to manage and ultimately end your addictive behavior. In Ron's case, he might have been able to discover what was so meaningful to him about the situation he found himself in that day, and therefore why he felt so overwhelmed when his colleagues faced with the same problem were not. To do this he would have to have spent time learning from previous instances when the urge to drink arose. He would have to have learned about what kind of powerlessness was intolerable for him. Then he could have seen what was happening at one o'clock that day and prevented the need to act altogether.

Let's take a closer look at how to end addiction, in seven steps.

PART II

The Steps

STEP 1

How to Know If You Have an Addiction

"I keep doing the same things too much, too often. Does that mean I have an addiction?" This question is at the heart of Step 1. Lots of people repeat behaviors like drinking, exercising, and shopping in a way they (or others) consider too much. But that does not necessarily mean they have an addiction. There are other possible causes of repetitive, even excessive behaviors. The best way to check whether any particular behavior is an addiction is to compare it with the description of addiction put forward in Part One.

The first question you might ask yourself is: When does my addictive act (or even just the thought of it) arise? Is it when you are feeling helpless about something—being insulted, left out, used or abused, ignored, hopeless, or any other feeling that for you leads to that intolerable sense of helplessness? Of course, you may not know what is setting off thoughts of your addictive act until you have a chance to think carefully about it. But if the behavior you are concerned about is triggered by this kind of emotional upset, it is much more likely to be a true addiction.

It will also help to compare your behavior with examples of *non-addiction* causes of repetitive behavior that I will describe below.

1. HABITS

Michelle was a coffee lover. She drank it morning, noon, and night, at home and at work. She would never dream of confusing café au lait with caffè latte. She could knowledgeably discuss the merits of French, Italian, and Viennese roasts. Indeed, in candid moments even she had to admit the sad truth. She was a coffee snob. However, she had been having trouble sleeping and lately her stomach was giving her trouble, too. When she talked to her doctor and told him how many cups she had each day he ordered her off coffee altogether, at least for a while. As far as Michelle was concerned he might as well have suggested she stick her hand in an electric socket for a few weeks.

But she tried. Oh, she simply had to have one cup in the morning, but that was it! Yet at 10:30 she knew. She always had a cup of coffee at 10:30. She looked at the clock on her desk: 10:30. She looked in her pocketbook for gum but there wasn't any. She looked around the room, then back at the clock: 10:31. "What's one cup?" she said as she stood up and headed for the exit. Lucky for her, she thought, the coffee shop was right next door.

———

Is this an addiction? Michelle was doing something that wasn't good for her. And she already had a history of doing it too much. Yet the key is not whether coffee was good for her or even whether she had too much of it. Michelle felt an urge to drink coffee both when she woke up and at 10:30 because she *always* had a cup of coffee at those times. Her coffee drinking wasn't driven by more important emotional issues. It was just a habit.

Habits are very different from addictions. They are automatic behaviors that don't have deeper meaning. Turning off the lights when leaving a room or reading the sections of a newspaper in a certain order are examples. Habits can be hard to break simply because they require attention at a time you aren't noticing what you're doing. In fact, not having to pay attention to what you're doing is a big part of what we mean by a habit, and a big part of what can make them so useful. If you had to pay attention to all the things you do by habit you'd have no time for anything else.

Besides having to pay attention to what you are doing, habits can of course be hard to break if you enjoy doing them. In fact, you may have developed that habit just because it was so pleasant, like having that cup of coffee at midmorning.

But as we all know, habits can be broken, and everyone has had to break some at one time or another. While this takes effort, it is not something that requires treatment. From a psychological standpoint, habits are superficial phenomena, only as deep as a scratch on your skin. How different that is from addictions, which arise as a (temporary) solution to problems with much deeper roots.

So, what happened to Michelle? She had a hard time giving up her coffee. But after a day of waffling, she did it. She loved coffee but it wasn't worth the risk to her health. Stopping was, for Michelle, a simple and rational decision to follow her doctor's advice. Did that mean she was a more rational human being than people with addictions? Certainly not. All it meant was that when it came to quitting coffee, she didn't have to deal with the complex and powerful feelings underlying addiction.

It isn't always easy to distinguish addictions from habits. To be sure of what you're dealing with it may be necessary to take some time to investigate whether there is something deeper driving the behavior. In later chapters I will discuss how to go about this self-investigation. But for now, if you wonder whether your behavior (or the behavior of someone you love) is an addiction, see if the pattern of behavior looks like a habit. Habits are linked with familiar situations, like the time of day or a regular activity. Michelle drank coffee at certain times. Someone else might have a cigarette with his morning coffee. Another person might have a glass of wine while relaxing at the end of the day, or get on the Internet to check favorite sites, or play a game. If the behavior in question is routine, not associated with any emotionally meaningful events, and—most important—if it's the result of simply *liking* a behavior, and not feeling that one *must* do it, then the behavior may just be a habit. People with true addictions also may at times say they repeat their addictive behaviors simply because they like them ("I like the taste of beer"), but usually you can tell the difference. People with addictions will fight hard to defend the behavior. Those with a habit may put up resistance, but are able to stop fighting back when presented with sensible reasons to stop.

2. PHYSICAL ADDICTION

Physical addiction is a way our bodies react to certain drugs, and it is utterly out of our control. For this reason, *physical* addiction can be a cause of repetitive behavior that looks like the kind of *psychological* addiction I have been describing. It needs to be carefully distinguished, however, because physical factors are of relatively little significance in understanding the nature and treatment of addiction. It is because of this that I call only psychological addiction "true" addiction. But how do you tell the difference between these two kinds of addictions?

The simplest way is to stop the behavior and see what happens. Stopping physical addiction is accomplished by not taking the drug long enough to allow your body to readjust to being without it (completing a withdrawal). Withdrawal is always unpleasant and for certain drugs can be quite dangerous. Depending on the drug, withdrawal may require medical supervision or hospitalization. (The most dangerous drugs to withdraw from are brain sedatives like alcohol, Xanax or Valium, and barbiturates. Narcotic withdrawal, despite all its discomfort, is not medically dangerous, and neither is withdrawal from "uppers" like cocaine or amphetamines, though these lead to a so-called crash in mood.) But as unpleasant as withdrawal can be, it is relatively easy compared with trying to give up an addiction that is based on the kinds of psychological issues described in Part One. Indeed, if all you have is a physical addiction, then after withdrawal (detoxification) your problem is basically over as long as you don't have a *psychological addiction* as well.

You may find this surprising, since in our culture the notion that people are controlled by their drugs (or "hooked") is a common myth. Yet, in the early 1980s millions of people quit smoking after the U.S. surgeon general issued a statement about the severe risks of smoking and required warning labels to be placed on cigarette packs. These millions had a physical dependence on nicotine, yet, like Michelle in the example above, they were able to stop smoking when they realized it was dangerous. Their experience shows that physical addiction (or *dependence*), by itself, is simply not a significant impediment to regaining control of your behavior. Physical dependence is just not a major factor in the problem of addiction.

Probably the most famous illustration of this point is a study done on the experience of soldiers in Vietnam.[2] The Vietnam War placed a huge number of men and women with no history of addiction into an enormously stressful setting where there was an easy supply of heroin. Many soldiers used enough heroin to become physically addicted. At this same time, back in the States,

[2] Robins, L., J. Helzer, and D. Davis, 1975. "Narcotic use in Southeast Asia and afterward." *Archives of General Psychiatry* 32: 955–61.

heroin addiction had become a major problem among the civilian population; treatment programs had proved largely unsuccessful, with nearly all heroin addicts going back to the drug after detoxification. So there was much concern about what would happen to the soldiers when they came home. Would they be "hooked" on heroin and unable to get off, like the stateside addicts?

Over 90 percent of these veterans, after returning home and being safely detoxified, never used heroin or another narcotic again. Why not? Having a physical addiction just isn't enough to make people continue to use a drug once they are withdrawn. These soldiers had used heroin because they were in a war, not because it afforded them a way to deal with important inner emotional issues. As with the cigarette smokers who dropped their habit in light of the surgeon general's warning, the veterans suffered only from physical addiction, so they were able to stop.

But the stateside folks who were using heroin did so because they had a different kind of addiction—a behavior compelled by psychological factors. Detoxifying them, by itself, didn't help. Treatment for them would have had to address the psychological basis of their problem.

For a clearer understanding of the relationship between true addiction and physical addiction, it's helpful to note that there are many addictions that have no physical dependence or withdrawal at all. Even some drug addictions are this way; for example, addictive use of marijuana and hallucinogens such as mushrooms has no associated physical addiction because these substances are incapable of producing physical dependence. And of course, there is no true physical addiction or withdrawal in addictions not involving drugs, like compulsive gambling, sexual addiction, or compulsive eating. Yet people regularly shift from drug to nondrug addictions and back. About 40 percent of compulsive gamblers also have alcoholism. It would not be possible for people to substitute nondrug addictions for drug addictions unless these activities all served the same function. As everyone who has suffered from one knows, nondrug addictions carry the same desperate urges to repeat them, and are just as capable of prevailing irrationally over concerns for one's own welfare (or the welfare of others) as drug addictions. In our society we have tended to focus on drug addiction, but that doesn't mean addiction is about drugs.

THE MOST COMMON MISUNDERSTANDING OF ADDICTION: THE "BRAIN DISEASE" MODEL

In recent years it has become popular to say that addiction is a kind of neurological illness, a "chronic brain disease." This idea comes from experiments in which rats were given large doses of narcotics for a long time, and then were found to seek more of the drug, even when simply exposed to cues that had been associated with the drug. This is a form of conditioned reflex, like Pavlov's famous experiment in which a bell rang every time a group of dogs were fed. The dogs learned to associate the bell with food, eventually salivating when the bell rang, even in the absence of food. They were conditioned to respond to the bell alone. In the recent experiments with rats and narcotics, rats were exposed to cues associated with a drug they'd been regularly administered. In response, they automatically sought the drug, as if the drug itself were present. Examination of the rats' brains showed that these cues produced the same response as the drug itself—releasing an excitatory chemical (a neurotransmitter called dopamine). On further examination, researchers found there had been changes in the anatomy of the rats' brains, making them extra sensitive to re-exposure—to either the drug or just the associated cues alone. In other words, in a vicious cycle, exposure to narcotics for a long time made the rats more likely to respond to additional exposure (to the drugs or just the cues) with further drug-seeking behavior. In light of these results, the experimenters concluded that addiction was a chronic brain disease that worked in people just the way it did in rats. If true, this would mean that addiction was caused by use of the very drugs a person used addictively, though it could not explain why people had begun to use them so much to begin with.

However, this theory turned out not to fit the facts in humans. When a group of ordinary people is exposed to high doses of narcotics for a long time, such as medically ill people, or the Vietnam soldiers I mentioned above, they become physically dependent (just like the rats); but, unlike the rats, once they are safely withdrawn from the drug, extremely few people become addicts. They do not have an automatic, conditioned response to the drugs or to environmental cues associated with the drug. People, it turns out, are different from rats.

The main difference is our big brains. We can process ideas, complicated feelings, and internal conflicts in ways a rat could never imagine. It is our complex psychology—our conflicts and defenses—which lead us to make individual choices for good or ill based on who we are. Ron Golding, whom we met in Part One, is a good example of this. When Ron decided to drink, there was no drug-related cue in his environment. He was at work. Not only that, when he decided to repeat his addictive behavior he was planning ahead—many hours ahead. His brain was not flooded with excitatory chemicals. In fact, once he decided on his plan for the future, he was able to calmly get down to work. Ron's addiction was completely different from the way addiction works in rats.

OTHER CAUSES OF BEHAVIORS THAT
LOOK LIKE ADDICTIONS

A few other sources of repetitive, excessive behavior that are *not* addictions are listed below (for a more detailed discussion of non-addiction issues, see my previous book, *The Heart of Addiction*). Consider if any of these might apply to you, or to whomever you are concerned about. But a word of caution: it is common for both a true addiction and some combination of factors like those below to be present at the same time. Be sure to give yourself a chance to watch the behavior for a while before concluding that it is not an addiction.

1. **Relationship pressure.** Sometimes people do things because their partners or their group is doing it. A wife may drink too much because her husband has alcoholism. She may feel left out of her husband's life when he is drinking, so she drinks with him. Or sometimes a person who has an addiction pressures his or her partner to join in. In teenage groups, doing something because "everyone" is doing it can be a powerful reason to participate. But none of these examples is an addiction.
2. **Special settings.** At the Thanksgiving dinner table Uncle Joe always gets drunk. This doesn't necessarily mean he has alcoholism. People are often influenced by their environment to behave outside their usual ways of acting. Uncle Joe's Thanksgiving tippling could be something of a tradition for him. If it were truly just that, he could stop it if it caused enough trouble. Settings can also be purposely created to encourage excessive behavior. Gambling casinos are a perfect example. They are built to encourage more gambling than you would do ordinarily. There are no clocks and no windows, so you can more

easily lose track of time. There are flashing lights and musical sounds to let you know that somebody somewhere in the building is winning. Often, there is free alcohol. This is not a gift. Gambling more than you intended under these circumstances does not mean you have a gambling addiction.

3. **Adolescence.** Teenagers routinely do excessive activities that range from merely outlandish to dangerous. When they are repeated, at times these can look very much like an addiction. The key here is to figure out whether these actions are part of normal adolescent rebellion (done because they're forbidden), or part of normal trying out of new identities (doing strange things to figure out who you are), or just normal adolescent belief in one's immortality ("Aw, Dad, you worry too much"). Distinguishing these causes from true addictions is often not so easy. Talking to your adolescent is always a good idea. But if you are still worried, then a consultation with somebody who understands both the psychological nature of addiction and the normal psychology of adolescence is your best bet.[3] I will return to the topic of teenage addiction in Part Three, "Living with Someone Who Has an Addiction."

If you've decided that you are dealing with a true addiction, the next step is to figure out what this means about you, and just as important, what it does *not* mean.

-----

[3] If you do this, remember that the consultation must respect the adolescent's privacy. You can tell your teen that you have to know if treatment is recommended, but the details discussed with the consultant won't be revealed to you.

STEP 2

How to Think about Yourself If You Have an Addiction

Once you recognize that you have an addiction one of the first issues you must face is how this leads you to feel about yourself. It is important to settle this issue now so it does not interfere with your determination or self-confidence as you move on to the rest of the steps toward breaking your addiction. For instance, you may feel like you have become a member of a new, separate group that has been given a very bad reputation: "addicts." But most people have mistaken ideas about addiction, so, too, they have mistaken ideas about those who suffer from them. For example:

- If people believe that addiction is due to being physically "hooked" on drugs, they may believe you created your own addiction. "If only you had not taken those drugs then you wouldn't have an addiction!" Of course, excessive use of drugs is just one form of displacement in addictions. It is neither the cause of addiction nor the basic reason an addiction persists.
- If people believe that addiction is a chronic brain disease, then they must consider you very different from themselves.

You are chronically and permanently disabled because of your damaged brain. How sad that you don't have a delightfully normal brain, like they do! As we've seen, there is considerable evidence that whatever changes may occur in brains during long-term use, these changes do not create addictions in humans.

• If people believe that "addicts" are weak willed, stupid, or lazy, then you may be stigmatized by those views. The psychological mechanism at work in addiction (as I hope is clear) has nothing whatever to do with weakness, stupidity, or laziness.

The fact is, if you suffer with an addiction you are not different at all from anyone else.

"But," you may argue, "not everyone has an addiction!" True enough, but there is an important response to that point: virtually everyone has a psychological or emotional problem of *some* kind. Many years ago there was a study in which everyone in a single geographic area was interviewed just to see how common it was to be "normal" (meaning, in this case, free of emotional troubles). The results were surprising, though they shouldn't have been. The study revealed that practically none of the subjects were normal; nearly everyone had psychological problems, as defined by the study, in one measure or another. Since an addiction is no more and no less than a psychological symptom—just one of many human mechanisms for dealing with emotional life—having an addiction places you squarely in the mainstream of humanity.

A particularly clear illustration of this occurs in cases where people replace addictive behavior with another psychological symptom that can perform the same function, as in the following story[4]:

---

[4] This vignette is drawn from: Dodes, L. M. "Compulsion and Addiction." 1966. *Journal of the American Psychoanalytic Association* 44: 815–35.

AMY

Amy Johnson had her marching orders. She wasn't in the military, but that's how life with her husband, William, usually felt. He was always busy with tasks and plans that seemed more important than her own, so she became his support staff. Of course, her daily duties might have been considered important—like being a mother to their three children (ages three-and-a half to seven), shopping, cooking, and taking care of more or less everything about their personal lives—but the couple both seemed to take for granted that these things were of lower priority. Then, there were the one or two things she liked to do for herself, but they were definitely on the bottom of the list.

Amy suffered with alcoholism. Her drinking had been a problem in their marriage for years. William's view was that she lacked the backbone to control herself. Why she didn't just do what she had to do, as he told himself *he* would have, and get it done without having to drink was beyond his understanding. He did care about Amy, but he had no interest at all in why she drank. Why should he? He had long ago decided it was simply a weakness of hers; he was actually something of a saint to put up with it.

On this particular day Amy's main order was to mail a certain letter at the post office for William. "This has to go out by noon," he had said. It was just the sort of directive that Amy obeyed nearly every day, only to follow the task by going directly to one of her several secret places in the house where she kept some wine. Drinking had always been a solution for the overwhelming helplessness she felt whenever she passively followed William's orders. But today turned out to be different.

Amy took the letter from William and walked out of the room. There was no thought of rebellion. In fact, she was thinking about how to arrange her morning to get to the post office and still do everything else. She walked into the kitchen and looked in the refrigerator to see what she needed to buy. Then she went to check on her youngest to make sure she was playing happily. Okay. She'd mail the letter now, bring the baby (they still called her the baby) with her, and be back in time for the next item on her list. She was about to tell her daughter that they were going out when she noticed she no longer had the letter in her hand. She turned around in a complete circle in the baby's room. Not there. She retraced her steps to the kitchen. It wasn't on the table, or on the counter. She walked back to where William had given her the letter. He was gone and there was no sign of the envelope either. She had lost it.

Amy was aware that losing the letter left her with a mix of feelings. On the one hand, this was a problem. The letter had to go out and it was her responsibility to get it out. On the other hand, there was something satisfying about having lost it. She stood there a moment. "Well," she said to herself, "nothing I can do about it now," and she went back to the kitchen to write down a shopping list. When she finished, she put the list in her purse, picked it up, and was about to collect her daughter when she noticed the missing envelope, right there near the toaster. "Huh!" she said out loud. She frowned at the envelope. "How did I miss that?" she thought.

Amy picked up the letter and went into the baby's room. "We're going to go to the store," she said. She held her daughter's hand as they walked back though the kitchen to the back door, where she went out, closed the door, and locked it from outside. On the way to her car she looked in her pocketbook to be sure she still had the shopping list. There it was. But no letter. She stopped. "Come on," she said to her daughter, "I have to go back inside a second." Once in the kitchen she looked again. Then she looked in the baby's room. Nope, the letter was gone. She had lost it again. Amy shrugged her shoulders, and went out with her daughter to shop. She did not drink that day.

———

What happened here? Usually Amy complied with her husband's demands, and then drank to reverse her helplessness about going along. This time, quite unconsciously, she found another way to deal with his demands: by losing his letter, she couldn't possibly mail it. This was a new way to assert herself.

Unconscious actions like Amy's misplacement of the letter are common in everyday life. They are actions that appear to allow a person's deeper feelings to "leak out." When they are unintentional words instead of behavior they are often called slips of the tongue, or sometimes Freudian slips.[5] Amy's behavioral "slip" of losing the letter was just like that. It was a psychological symptom that expressed her deeper feelings. She couldn't consciously allow herself to defy or even resist William's order, but she did exactly that through the new symptom of forgetfulness. She didn't drink that day because she didn't need to: losing William's letter had done the same job.

Amy had therefore substituted a new psychological symptom for her addiction. This was only possible because addictions are themselves psychological symptoms. They are mechanisms of the mind such as anybody could have.

OTHER REASONS WHY HAVING AN ADDICTION MAKES YOU NO DIFFERENT FROM ANYONE ELSE

- **The drive in addictions is normal.** Addictive actions are often sought out and performed with great intensity, which can strike people as unusual. But remember (from Part One) that the

---

[5] The technical name for such unconsciously determined behavior is "parapraxis."

strength of the drive in addiction is actually quite normal. It is just that other people can't see the feeling of being overwhelmingly trapped that you have in those moments. So the drive to act that they *do* see doesn't make sense to them. It's good to keep in mind that if you and they were trapped together in a cave-in (our conventional example of a helpless situation), you would all be furiously pounding on the rocks just the same.

- **Addictions are just compulsions.** You probably have noticed that while talking about addictions I have described them as compulsive. Some addictions even have the word "compulsive" in their names, like "compulsive gambling." "Compulsions," as a diagnostic group, are basically identical to addictions. They are behaviors that are strongly driven, repetitive, and difficult to stop even if you wish you could. Yet most compulsions have never suffered the indignities heaped on addictions. Having a compulsion to place the papers on your desk so they are all parallel, or feeling compelled to plump your pillows just so every night, or read every book until the very last page are hardly reasons to be singled out as different from your friends and neighbors. Compulsions are so common, in fact, that they are often taken for granted, or are at worst a source of good-hearted humor. Compulsions also operate the same way as addictions. They, too, are driven by an intense need and are displaced behaviors that arise when direct expression of this drive is seen as forbidden. Here is an example:

  A man who had lifelong anger toward his father, but could not allow himself to express it, felt compelled to make undermining comments about his boss at work—without knowing why he repeatedly did something so potentially self-destructive. His compulsion was driven by the same factors as an addiction: he felt helpless to assert himself with his father and he displaced this need to a substitute action (toward someone who also made a good stand-in for his father). If, in place of consistently making rude comments about his boss, he had taken a handful of pills, then this would commonly be called an addiction instead of a compulsion.

Addictions are no more or less than compulsions. They are so much alike, one wonders why people haven't seen this clearly before. The misconception that drugs and their physical effects play an important role in addiction has made it hard to see addiction's psychological foundations. And further, it has obscured the link between addictions and other psychologically-based compulsions.

- **Addictions don't mean you are sicker than anyone else.** Unfortunately, people tend to judge the nature and seriousness of a symptom not by what is inside a person's mind but by its consequences in the world. Since addictions often cause tremendous losses to the people who have them, as well as to those around them, they are viewed as more serious emotional problems. But there is not a good correlation between the seriousness of emotional trouble and the seriousness of its consequences. There are some quite troubled people whose main symptoms are completely hidden from view. Having an addiction, even if it is serious, does not mean you must be sicker than anyone else.

- **Treatment for addictions is no different than treatment for other psychological symptoms.** If having an addiction doesn't mean you are different from the rest of humanity, it also means you can be treated like anyone else. For years, unfortunately, some therapists felt that people with addictions should not be treated in psychotherapy because they were too sick. That was a tragedy. The fact is, if you have an addiction you are just as capable of understanding yourself as anyone else.

Another still-common myth is that addictions should be treated separately, before considering the overall emotional issues facing the individual. Can you imagine going to see a therapist for a compulsion to wash your hands and being told, "I'll be glad to treat you, but you first have to get treatment to stop washing your hands"? A variant of this is to be told, "I'll treat you, but you have to simultaneously see someone else to deal with your addiction." Old attitudes like these are based on the idea that addictions are so different from other problems that they cannot, even should not, be talked about and explored like any other symptom. The opposite is the case.

Because addictions are efforts to deal with the most important emotional issues of your life, it is impossible to understand them without understanding yourself as a person. Likewise, it is extremely useful to explore the emotional factors that precipitate addictive behavior; understanding these factors provides a shortcut, a "royal road" to understanding yourself.

STEP 3

Recognizing the Key Moment
in Addiction

When people think about an addiction, their own or someone else's, they tend to focus on its devastating effects. Probably the single most common question put to people with addictions is "Don't you realize what you're doing to yourself?" The second most common question is probably "Don't you realize what you're doing to those around you?" Often enough this is said in anger, but there is also the idea that if only you could get these people with addictions to realize what they're doing, then they would finally change their behavior.

Having an addiction doesn't mean you have lost your memory or your ability to think. In the past thirty years I have seen very few people with addictions who did not have a very clear idea indeed of what they had done to themselves and others. Most of the time they are all too aware of this and are filled with regret. Focusing on the effects of addiction is not helpful either for yourself or somebody you care about. Too often, it results in more shame for the person with addiction and more estrangement between that person and whoever is doing the "reminding."

By devoting time to the consequences of behavior it is also easy to overlook the fact that these consequences were not intended. We already know that addictions are a solution to an internal problem, not an attempt to create external problems for oneself or others.

There is an even more fundamental problem with spending your time and effort thinking about the effects of addiction. The more time you spend on that, the less time you spend doing something truly valuable: looking at the *causes* of addiction.

DON'T FOCUS ON YOUR ADDICTIVE BEHAVIOR ITSELF

Paying a lot of attention to addictive behavior itself is also not a particularly good use of your time. By the time you are in the act, the drive in addiction is generally too powerful to manage. Here's a case that illustrates this problem:

JAMES

James couldn't stop buying lottery tickets. He had a favorite convenience store that sold them, one he liked because it seemed as though every week they had a new sign saying how much money had been won by people who had purchased tickets there. His gambling addiction had been terrible for him. He was not a wealthy man to start, and he could have badly used the hundreds of dollars he had been losing each month. He was determined to stop. So he made an elaborate plan.

First, he was going to avoid his favorite store, which was near his apartment building, by walking out of his way on his trip home from the bus stop after work. Second, when he did have to go to the store to pick up essentials (he didn't have a car so it was hard to shop elsewhere) he was going to stay away from the table that was set up to fill out lottery ticket numbers. If that didn't work, he carried a list with him that showed the amounts he had lost in each of the previous four weeks and he was determined to look at it before finally buying the ticket.

This system worked perfectly for two days.

On the third day, he went to the store to get some milk. He walked right over to the lottery table, filled out a ticket form playing his favorite number, took it to the counter, had the ticket printed by the machine behind the counter, and paid for it. Later, when asked about what had gone through his mind, he said, "I just thought, 'Fuck it. I'm going to get this ticket.'"

After his experience in the store James redoubled his efforts. Now he changed his walking route altogether. He found another small convenience store in which he could shop, one that didn't sell lottery tickets. He was doing well for a little while, but he still thought about buying the tickets and he noticed that when he didn't buy them he felt anxious and irritable. A day or two later, while he was in the new convenience store, he stopped to buy a pack of cigarettes. He hadn't smoked in ten years but, lighting up, he found the tension drain from his body. It was wonderful. In fact, it relieved his tension just as well as buying lottery tickets had done. Within another week he was smoking a pack a day.

Several weeks later he saw his doctor for a routine checkup. "Nothing's wrong, Doc," he said when they shook hands. His doctor smiled, "Good to hear." Then the doctor went through his system review checklist: problems with head, eyes, nose, throat, heart, breathing, etc. James quickly answered: no, no, no, fine, fine. All went well until the smoking question. The doctor was taken aback.

"I thought you didn't smoke," he said.

"Yeah, well, I didn't but I just started up."

The doctor stared at him. "For God's sake, why?"

James shrugged uncomfortably. "I don't know," he finally said.

———

As James's experience illustrates, another reason it doesn't pay to focus too closely on an addictive act itself is because it can change. We know that the particular form of an addiction is just a displacement—an action that gives a sense of empowerment in the face of helplessness—and that this displacement can shift. James had prepared as well as he could for buying lottery tickets, but he was blindsided by the move to cigarettes.

Ultimately, focusing on addictive behavior itself is unwise because, quite simply, this behavior is not the issue. For the past few thousand years people have looked at addiction and seen the form it takes—some behavior—as the enemy. Even today, some treatments deal with addictive behavior as an enemy to be stamped out. But this is a mistake. Since addictive behavior is nothing more or less than a symptom, you have to shift your gaze past the behavior, to a point in time before you are doing it, a point closer to the *cause* of the behavior, rather than the behavior itself.

Of course, as you find yourself in the midst of an addictive behavior there is nothing wrong with trying to stop it. Certainly, if you stop drinking after just one drink that will reduce the consequences of drinking, if you stop gambling after the first bet it will reduce your losses, and if you stop eating after the first piece of cake you will improve your health. That's wonderful. But stopping on any one occasion doesn't affect the process of thought and feeling that led to the action. It isn't the solution to your addiction. If our goal is to end addiction, rather than just fight it forever, then we must look beyond the behavior.

The ability to stop in the middle of performing addictive acts, while obviously good for limiting their damage, is also not very useful for predicting the future. People with alcoholism regularly prove to themselves they can have "just one," then go overboard later. So if you are able to stop in the middle of doing your addictive acts, that's great. But it would be dangerous to assume that being able to stop now means you will always be able to stop. In fact, without working out the need to perform addictive acts, people typically remain highly vulnerable to relapse. If you are not able to stop in the middle, that doesn't mean you are weak or that your addiction is beyond your control. It only shows that you have not yet worked out the reasons you have your addiction and how they lead you down that path. That's okay, since you're only on Step 3!

FOLLOW YOUR BEHAVIORS BACK TO THE KEY MOMENT

As we know, the addictive act is only a final step in a chain of precipitating thoughts. Indeed, all actions are preceded by thoughts, feelings, and sometimes earlier behaviors that lead to the final result. Knowing the stops along this path will help to address the final behavior sooner, at a point when the addictive drive is less intense. Here is an example:

MARJORIE

Everyone in Marjorie Fuller's family loved her. At forty-two years old she had never been married but she counted herself lucky to have close sisters and brothers. In fact, as the oldest of the five siblings she had always felt it was her job to keep her younger brothers and sisters happy and close. Whether that was realistic or not, she continued to feel it was her responsibility into adulthood. When there was a family get-together, she was the one who did all the planning. She had a large enough home to accommodate everyone, and when she had guests overnight she always made sure she was up first to make breakfast. After eating, she encouraged the others to sit in her backyard and enjoy the weather while she cleaned up.

At some time in the past, the next-oldest sister used to offer to help clean up on these occasions, but Marjorie insisted she could take care of everything. After a while even this sister took for granted that Marjorie wanted to serve them and gave up trying. Marjorie's two brothers had always taken this for granted, since childhood, and now as adults their wives smiled and thanked Marjorie for being such a lovely hostess, but seemed allergic to the concepts of washing dishes, shopping, planning, or cooking.

Marjorie herself believed she just wanted to serve others. "It's wrong to be selfish," she would say. If questioned about this she would add, "What kind of world would it be if people just looked out for themselves?" The idea that there might be a middle position between only serving others and paying at least some attention to her own wishes seemed not to have occurred to her. On the surface, Marjorie appeared to be unconflicted and comfortable in her self-assigned role as caregiver. She was clear in her own mind that she was leading her life the way she should, the right way.

But all was not right in her world, and the most obvious sign of that was that Marjorie consumed an enormous quantity of pills. She kept stashes of Xanax, Valium, and Klonopin that she had obtained from several doctors over the years, making sure that none of the doctors knew about any of the others. She took them whenever she felt "nervous." The result was that for all her efforts to take care of others she was well known among her friends and family to be utterly unreliable when it came to keeping appointments. She was often jumpy and depressed. She had needed to be hospitalized on two occasions, once after collapsing on the floor in a stupor and the other time when she had a seizure. (She had collapsed when she lost track of the pills she had already taken and had taken some more. Her seizure occurred after one of her attempts to abruptly stop using her pills cold turkey.)

Marjorie was well aware of her problem with drugs but saw it mainly as a personal failure to do things right. When asked about her pill abuse she said, "I shouldn't do it. I know that. It hurts other people. When I missed that appointment with my sister to help her shop for a new sofa, it was terrible. She had to go to the furniture store alone. She hates that. What kind of sister does that?"

Of course, Marjorie was aware that her drug use also created problems for herself, some of them serious. But she shrugged that off. Those problems only involved her being hurt, and who really cared about that?

It was a warm September weekend when she had a group of family over to her house, again. She had been safely off her pills for a couple of weeks at that point and was feeling pretty good. It was always exciting for her to plan affairs. She liked to think about who would want to do what, about what people liked to eat (it was routine for her to prepare several choices for each meal, like a restaurant), and she was shopping and fussing for a couple of days in advance. Her two sisters and both brothers and all their spouses and children arrived Friday afternoon and she fed them that evening, then breakfast, lunch, and dinner Saturday, and Sunday brunch. Throughout the weekend until they left late Sunday afternoon she arranged games and activities. When they all left, she smiled and waved, then turned back into her house. "I think they had a wonderful time," she thought to herself standing on her front porch, before turning and walking inside.

She walked right over to the bathroom medicine cabinet, un-screwed the top of one of the drugstore vials and poured two oval pills into her hand, popped them in her mouth, filled a small glass, and washed them down. Over the next six hours, she would have four more and then fall into a black sleep.

Marjorie's strict sense of duty to take care of others was like living in a prison. It is not easy trying to be a saint, and that is just what she imposed on herself. Since expressing her own needs—or even limiting the amount she did for others—was morally unacceptable for her, she was trapped.

But somewhere inside—where she could not, or would not, let herself see—was a firestorm of resentment at living in this trap. It had to burst out, and when she took her pills late Sunday afternoon, it finally did. By the time she was standing at the medicine cabinet it was too late to stop the explosion.

Marjorie believed that taking her pills was a kind of afterthought to the weekend. But that was not so. There had been several times while she was serving her guests on Friday and Saturday that the idea of taking pills entered her mind. She had pushed those thoughts aside quickly while her guests were there. She only remembered them much later, when she was asked specifically about whether drugs had entered her mind while taking care of her guests.

Clearly, her pill use was not an afterthought. She had not taken any drugs earlier in the weekend, and she hadn't even seriously considered taking them. But the thought was there, and it is truly the thought that counts when it comes to dealing with addiction.

What if she had paid attention to her thought? That could have changed everything. Instead of marching directly to her medicine cabinet after waving good-bye Sunday afternoon, driven beyond words to have a pill *right then*, she might have been able to reflect on why her drugs were coming to mind. As we will discuss later in the book, she would have had the opportunity to think through what she knew about her addiction, and had a chance to resolve the need for it. And if she could have thought about this *before* she had pushed herself to serve even more, entertain even more, and be the jovial host even more, she might have had a chance to stop the sequence that was building the pressure that would inevitably lead to the overwhelming compulsion to use drugs.

But let's look further back. Her fleeting thoughts of taking pills while she was entertaining her guests earlier in the weekend were not the first time they had come to mind. On Friday morning before anyone arrived, while she was getting the house ready, she had thought of taking some pills. As soon as that thought came to mind, she had an image in her mind of being drugged as she tried to greet her guests. She was determined not to embarrass herself again. But she never considered what her thought might mean, or even that it would be useful to consider it. Thinking about drugs was dangerous and wrong, she believed. It was best to push those thoughts away as fast and hard as possible.

Certainly, Marjorie missed a chance to deal with her addictive urge even before her guests were there, on Friday. So was that the optimal point at which she could have focused her attention on her own thoughts? No. The very first time the thought of pills had entered her mind was not Friday, or even Thursday. It was Wednesday, when she began to plan her shopping for the weekend, a full four days before she took a pill. It was when she sat down at her kitchen table and, in her usual organized way, took out a notepad and began to make a list of things she needed to do. The process that culminated in an addictive act on Sunday had begun on Wednesday.

———

Imagine what Marjorie could have done if she had paid attention to that very first moment. At that time, there was the least drive to perform her addiction, so she was in the very best position to think about it. She could have done two critical things.

First, from a practical standpoint, she still had options about how to handle the weekend. Were there any ways to make it easier for herself so she did not build up all that rage at the trap she was about to step into? (I will come back to this point later.)

Just as important, at that first moment, she had the chance to understand her addiction in a new way. Why? Because at that moment—when she was furthest from her addictive behavior— she was closest to the *cause* of her addiction. The addiction itself, whether it is drinking, taking pills, eating, or compulsively looking at pornographic Web sites is always at the end of the chain of causality. The first step in that chain is the thought of doing the act.

The key moment in addiction is when the thought of it first comes to mind. This may be hours or even days before the addictive act occurs.

As in Marjorie's case, recognizing this key moment may not be simple. Here is a different example:

BRIAN

Brian had a sexual addiction and he knew it. He watched pornography on his computer at his desk for hours every day. Unfortunately, he also worked at a regular job as a research librarian every day, which meant that his employer, a major university, was not getting his full attention. Brian had performance reviews scheduled every six months, but because he never seemed to be getting enough work done in time for each of these reviews his boss had pushed up their frequency. Now Brian had to go in and show what he had accomplished every month. He knew he was on shaky ground at this job, and if he lost it, it would be his third strike. He had already lost two other good jobs because of poor performance, also due to his time watching pornography.

Brian was a very smart man and this had helped him keep the positions he had for as long as he did. His employers kept giving him the benefit of the doubt because they could see he knew the job and they saw his potential. In fact, more than one employer had tried to take him aside and ask if there was something wrong at home that might be distracting him, or if he needed some time off. The fact was that Brian's inability to complete a task on time and move on to the next one was a complete mystery to those who hired him.

It was not a mystery to Brian, of course, and he had tried everything he could to limit his pornography watching. His primary defense against his addiction was to be a step ahead of it. This was actually a very good idea, as we've seen in Marjorie's case above. Catching the addictive process early is critical. But what Brian meant by staying ahead of his addiction was to catch it early and kill it. In fact, he thought his addiction was like a bug, and his job was to exterminate it. When he was in his early twenties he had lived in an apartment colonized by cockroaches. He had taken to prowling stealthily through the apartment before going to bed each night, a can of roach-killing spray in each hand, ready to blast anything that showed itself. If he could catch them when they first showed themselves, he believed he would prevent them from taking over. This procedure never seemed to diminish the population of insects. But that didn't deter Brian. He rather liked the idea that he was muscling up to the invaders and drawing a line in the sand. They were numerous and ugly, but he was tough.

This process didn't work well for his addiction either. For the first few days after a performance review, Brian generally worked a bit better. But after the second day of staying on course he thought to himself, "Okay, I'm going to be prepared this time before it gets to me." He took a deep breath and knitted his brow. "All right, I'm ready. THERE WILL BE NO PORN TOMORROW!" He held his breath a moment and his look would have frightened any enemy, whether insect or pornographic Web site, that gazed upon it. However, the next day at work he watched several of his usual pornography sites for four hours. Afterward he felt defeated, again. Maybe he wasn't as tough as he thought, he said to himself miserably.

Brian's problem was that he didn't recognize the key moment for what it was. He thought that he was staying ahead of the game by declaring that he was not going to watch pornography. What he missed was that when he had the thought of *not* watching it, that meant he was already thinking about watching it. His thought, "I'm going to be prepared this time," was a bit like locking the barn door after the cows have left. He thought expressing his determination would prevent traveling down the road toward his addiction. Actually, it was the key moment *in* his addiction. It was the time to listen to himself, realize he had taken Step 1 already, and think through why his addictive process had started once again.

Brian believed that he could defeat his addiction by outsmarting it and out-toughing it. But his addiction wasn't the enemy.

He had no enemy.

What he had was a need to watch pornography, a symptom that could potentially be understood and mastered. Rather than fighting it like a bug, he needed to see it as part of himself, learn about it, understand it, and find ways to manage it. Locating that key moment would have been his first step in doing that.

Sometimes finding and identifying the key moment is especially tricky. Here is a short example:

STEVEN

Steven suffered with alcoholism. He had decided to stop drinking on many occasions but was never able to stick with it. It was a Saturday and he was looking in the refrigerator for something to eat. There was nothing. He picked up his keys and went out to his car. There were a couple of supermarkets within easy driving distance. The closest one was just a few minutes away, but he compared it in his mind to another one that was located in a large mall. "I probably need other things," he thought. "I'll check out the mall while I'm there." Having decided this, he nodded his head even though he was by himself.

Steven knew this mall. He shopped quickly for a few items in the supermarket, then left it by the exit leading to the other stores. He knew there was a liquor store at the end of the corridor, just on the right. He walked down there, bought a bottle of his usual brand of whiskey, retraced his steps through the supermarket to his car, and drove home. When he arrived he put away the groceries and the bottle and sat down in front of his TV to watch the baseball game. By the third inning, he had gotten up, opened the bottle, and was watching along with the first of several tall straight whiskeys he would have that day.

———

So when was the key moment for Steven's addiction? He must have thought about walking down that corridor toward the liquor store before he did it. Maybe that thought marked the key moment. Or perhaps it was in the supermarket when he decided to walk through the exit leading to the stores, rather than turn around and go out to his car. No, that couldn't be the key moment, since he had chosen this market precisely because he also wanted to visit other stores. The plan all along was to go to the other stores. Walking out of the supermarket into the mall wasn't a key moment. Doing that had been decided before Steven even left home.

Aha.

The key moment in Steven's addiction that day was long before he got to the liquor store, or to the supermarket. It wasn't even a time when he *thought* about drinking. It was the moment he chose to go to the supermarket that was near the liquor store. In that moment, he had taken the first step toward the drinking he would do a couple of hours later.

Steven had been able to conceal from himself this first key step because, unlike Marjorie and Brian, he never did have a conscious thought of drinking. He made up an explanation for why he had to go by the liquor store (he *rationalized* it) without ever consciously becoming aware of the reason he chose to go there.

So, we have to make a small modification in the rule for key moments:

The key moment in the chain of thoughts, feelings, and acts leading to an addictive behavior may be a decision to take an action that brings you closer to the addictive behavior, rather than a conscious thought about the addictive act itself.

Because the addictive act never comes to mind, these key moments can be harder to spot. In order to see them clearly, Steven—and the others we've met in this chapter—would have to recognize how they kept themselves from knowing their own true motivations. The ways people fool themselves can be called their defensive styles. Knowing your own defensive style is an essential tool to avoid blindly walking down the path to addiction. Learning this tool is the next step in breaking addiction.

How You Keep Yourself from Seeing the Addiction ahead of You

In the last chapter we saw that there is a key moment in addiction, and that it is when the thought of doing your addictive act first comes to mind. We also saw that this moment can be concealed because *you* can be an expert at keeping it from your awareness.

It is also likely that you can conceal from yourself later steps on the path toward your addictive act. Marjorie's key moment, for example, occurred long before she took her pills, when she was sitting at her kitchen table on a Wednesday planning her party for the upcoming weekend. But even after that she had fleeting thoughts of the pills on Friday and Saturday before finally taking them on Sunday. Each time she had those thoughts she pushed them out of her mind. But each of those times was an opportunity to recognize her march toward her addiction before it became overwhelming.

Wouldn't it be great if Marjorie had a way to know she was on the path to her addictive act even if she was trying to ignore it? If only there were signs or signals that could alert her.

It turns out that everyone has his or her own signs that indicate they are marching down that path. Of course, the signs for one person might be very different from those for anyone else. But all you need to know are your own signs.

These signs are not around you. They are not about being in a situation in which you are likely to use drugs or gamble or eat compulsively, even though it is important to recognize those situations as risky. The kinds of signals I am talking about are not around you because they are *in* you. They are ways that you deal with distress.

People have habitual ways of dealing with anxiety, sadness, fear, anger, and other feelings. These emotional defenses are pretty much permanent aspects of their personalities—techniques settled upon early in life to deal with emotions. Because these ways are so settled, once you recognize your own emotional defenses for managing difficult feelings, they can be used as signposts, or even warning signals.

In Marjorie's case, she consciously—intentionally—tried to push her thoughts of taking pills out of her mind. But this wasn't the only time she had done this. It was in fact one of her top techniques for dealing with thoughts she believed she should not have. It was how she had dealt with feeling attracted to certain men she believed were unsuitable for her. When she found herself imagining a relationship with them, she pushed those thoughts out of her mind. This did not work much better than her attempts to push away thoughts of taking pills. But the important point is that she was using the same technique.

Let's say that some years ago Marjorie had confided in a friend that this was what she did when she was trying to avoid her attraction to some men. Here's how a conversation between them might look. The two women have just sat down in a coffee shop and ordered coffees.

FRAN: Marjorie, you look distracted.

MARJORIE: Yeah, I am. I'm having a busy day. Mmm, this coffee smells good. Oh, by the way, I ran into that guy I told you about, Gary. I'm just not comfortable around him.

FRAN: I thought from the way talked about him that you liked him.

MARJORIE: Don't say that. I don't want to like him.

FRAN: Why not?

MARJORIE: He's not right for me. We're different in every way.

FRAN: Well, I know you said that before, but I got the impression that you were interested.

MARJORIE: No, I don't want to even think about him.

FRAN (*taking a sip of coffee, then setting it down*): Easier said than done.

(*Marjorie looks vaguely around at the other tables in the shop.*)

FRAN: You know, Gary is probably what's distracting you.

MARJORIE: No he isn't. I'm just having a busy day.

FRAN: You always say that! It concerns me. Maybe he really is on your mind. You should pay attention to that.

MARJORIE: Look, I put him out of my mind. He's just not on my mind.

FRAN: And just how do you do that?

MARJORIE: What do you mean?

FRAN: How do "put him out of your mind"? I've never been able to do that when I like a guy.

MARJORIE: I just tell myself not to think about it. It's self-control.

FRAN (*laughs*): You just tell yourself not to think about it? And that works?

MARJORIE: Sure it does.

FRAN: I don't know, Marge. I don't think it's possible.

(*Marjorie thinks for a while.*)

MARJORIE: Well, it works for me. (*Pause.*) For a while, anyway.

FRAN: Right! Then you get all distracted because it hasn't really gone away.

MARJORIE (*shrugs her shoulders*): Maybe.

———

What if Marjorie took her friend's comments seriously? What if she gave some real attention to the way she tried to push out of mind thoughts that were actually important to her, just because they were uncomfortable? She might notice, too, that trying to push them away didn't work so well. In fact, when Marjorie said she was having a busy day it was perfectly true. What she didn't appreciate was that she was busy trying to not think about what she was thinking about. That can be both distracting and exhausting.

If Marjorie recognized her tendency to deal with uncomfortable thoughts by trying to push them out of her mind, think how different things could have been the weekend she abused her pills. In the week leading up to her family's visit, when the thought of taking pills crossed her mind, along with the effort to push that thought away, she might have stopped short. "I'm doing it again!" she could have thought. "I'm trying to block my thoughts. I know what that means. I have to pay attention to this idea I'm trying to push out of mind. It isn't just a passing thought to be whisked away. It's important. If I don't think about it I may succeed in burying it. But it isn't going away. It's going to come back to bite me." Instead of barely noticing the key moment in the path to her pills, Marjorie would have recognized it for what it was.

Defensive styles vary. People have different methods of creating "blind spots." Consider another case we looked at in the last chapter:

Steven rationalized that he needed to go to a supermarket in a mall, telling himself he needed other items available there. But he actually chose that market because the mall had a liquor store. He couldn't recognize the key moment on the path to his addiction because it was buried by his rationalization. Steven often used rationalizations when he felt driven to do something that he also had misgivings about.

He was a big football fan; during football season he watched college games on Saturday and NFL games on Sunday. It was one of many factors that led to his divorce six years earlier. During his marriage, he often found himself torn between wanting to have peace with his wife and watching his beloved games. On more than one occasion he walked into the TV room and flipped on the set. "I just want to catch the score," he said to his wife each time. Despite long experience with his own behavior, he repeatedly convinced himself that this was true, that he would just find out the score.

His wife, however, was never fooled by this rationalization. "You're going to be in there *watching*," she said.

"No, no, I just want to see how the game is going," Steven invariably answered.

A few minutes later, his wife would call in, "You get the score yet?"

Steven hesitated. "Well, yes, but it's almost halftime. I just want to see what happens before the half. There are only five minutes left on the clock."

His wife, who knew nothing about football and cared less, did know, however, that five minutes of game time could mean fifteen or more minutes of TV time. She also knew that Steven knew this, but talking to him about it never did much good, at least in the heat of the moment. Steven's capacity to rationalize doing what he was driven to do was an ongoing feature of their marriage, and it was a factor in her eventual decision to seek a divorce.

But what if Steven had learned more about the way his mind worked? What if he had taken time to think about the ways he dealt with situations like watching football games? He might have said to himself, "I know I can talk myself into doing what I feel like doing, even when I know better. Problem is, I'm smart. I can come up with really convincing reasons to do things. But let's face it, those reasons are baloney. They're excuses to do what I was going to do anyway."

If Steven ever had this conversation with himself, he would have been better prepared for his decision to go to the mall. Knowing he had alcoholism, he might have anticipated he would come up with some rationalization to arrange to have a drink. Like Marjorie, he could have been prepared to recognize the key moment in his path to drinking because it was likely to involve his usual defensive style.

Here are a couple of other examples in which knowing your defensive style could help to catch an addiction at the key moment:

KEVIN

Kevin Lewis prided himself on his ability to think things through. The more difficult things became, the more he relied on his thinking.

He thought of himself as a turtle. When danger lurked, he just pulled in his head and pondered the situation for as long as he needed, sure that he would figure it out. Those around him marveled at his calm. He was, in fact, a good man to have with you when everyone was starting to panic. And as the manager of a small department at his company he often had to solve problems.

The downside was that he was slow to reach conclusions. There were times that a little panic would have helped. He didn't seem to hear those around him when they reminded him that the clock was ticking.

Kevin withdrew partly for the reason he knew: he was a good thinker and he liked to have peace and quiet to do that. He was also motivated to work hard to figure out how to deal with problems since he felt good about himself when he solved them. It was an important part of his self-esteem.

But that also meant that each time he was presented with a problem, it was a threat. If he couldn't solve it, his self-esteem suffered. This was a deeper reason why he was so slow. He had to go over his ideas in his mind again and again to be sure there were no flaws before showing them to the world. When people became impatient with him he ignored them, because it was more important to him to get it right.

Kevin had always been distant from others. People mostly liked him, but nobody could say he or she was close to him. In the best of times, when he was least anxious, he could joke with colleagues and be relaxed. The turtle head was out. But because he had deeper questions about himself, he couldn't let people in too far. The threat to his self-esteem from having to correctly solve problems was an example of his underlying sense of vulnerability. For all his outward calm, Kevin was often anxious. Deep inside he saw himself as fragile and weak, unable to exert control in the world. He had come to think of himself as a turtle not just because he could pull inside to his thinking when he felt under threat. It was also because he believed he needed a shell. There was always a threat.

Kevin was a compulsive gambler. He gambled the way he ran the rest of his life: he figured it out. He gambled mainly on horse races and he worked at knowing everything there was to know about each horse. He knew how it ran in sloppy conditions and on hard tracks. He knew whether it was better at longer distances or shorter ones. He knew about the jockeys. He was as expert as you could be without walking around the paddocks and examining each animal.

Unfortunately, despite all this knowledge, Kevin lost money regularly at the track. There were a couple of realistic reasons for this. First, it was a sporting event. If the outcome could reliably be predicted, then they wouldn't have to run the race. But more important, he was betting against the odds. These were set according to the way bets were placed at the track. When favorites ran, most people bet on them, resulting in unfavorable odds: you could always lose everything you bet, but if you won you would win only a little bit. Between the risks of things not turning out as expected and the odds, it was easy to lose money at the track.

But Kevin had even more losses than others, because he bet compulsively. He *had* to bet, which interfered with his usual judgment. He bet more than he could afford and he became all the more desperate—and bet more—when he did lose.

So he had tried to stop. For a while he had succeeded. He didn't go to the track, and he didn't read the daily racing form or the results in the papers. He felt better and his life was going better because he was not losing money.

Then a couple of things happened. First, there was a big problem at work. His boss, the section director, wanted to make an organizational change that required Kevin to downsize his department and merge it with another one. It wasn't clear who would run the newly combined department, but Kevin and his counterpart in the other department were supposed to work with each other during the process. Each man would work on decreasing his personnel while simultaneously liaising with the other to be sure the combined department had people with all the necessary skills.

Kevin liked problem solving, but that was when he could do it his usual way, by himself. Having to work with someone else with equal power—especially someone who had his own people to protect and his own agenda for the combined department—tormented him. With this arrangement it would be impossible for Kevin to implement his own solutions. Yet implementing his own solutions was very important to him. It meant he was in control, able to handle things, and that he was a highly competent man who could manage any threat.

He withdrew more than usual. Rather than working with his counterpart he sat in his office trying to figure out a way to control the result. There was no way to do it. The nature of the problem was that it had to be a coordinated effort, and inevitably a compromise. The more he worked on it, the more Kevin became obsessed with figuring it out. The turtle was completely inside his shell.

Kevin had never paid much attention to his long history of pulling away from others to figure things out on his own as his style of dealing with anxiety. Being the way he was just seemed a reasonable way to deal with life.

If he had been aware that this withdrawal was a defensive pattern to manage anxiety, rather than just a sensible method of figuring things out, then the unusual degree of distance he was now creating would have been like waving a red flag. He would have noticed it and stopped long enough to think about what it meant—that he was under a great deal of stress. He knew his stress was related to the merger, of course. But with this degree of withdrawal, he would realize that there had to be something more than the realistic problems the merger created. He might have been able to see that what was bothering him went beyond the merger itself. And, if he had gotten to know himself better, he might have realized that the trouble at work represented a challenge to his need to be in control of his world. He might even have recalled that this issue had a long history in his life.

If he had been aware of his defensive pattern he might have been able to step out of it and consider what was really bothering him. His defensive style could have been a signpost rather than a blockade to knowing why he felt so threatened.

But he didn't think about his defensive style. So he was unprepared for the next problem that cropped up almost immediately. That was his gambling.

Kevin was struggling with his work problem when he came across a horse-racing story in the sports pages of his newspaper. This wasn't a listing of racing results, which he had been avoiding. It was an article about a major upcoming race with a big purse. He recognized the article immediately as just what he was trying to ignore. Well, he had seen it now so he couldn't pretend he hadn't. What should he do?

He began to work the problem with his mind. Because it was a big race, he knew about almost all the horses that were entered. He felt he knew a lot about this race and what it took to win it. There were a couple of horses that were considered favorites, but everyone seemed to agree that this year many of them had a shot. That meant it was unusually hard to predict who would win. And that was a point in Kevin's favor. With no obvious choices for the average bettor to pick, driving down the odds, someone who had more knowledge would have an advantage. Kevin was that person; he was sure of it.

Of course, he had stopped gambling. But this was an unusual opportunity. He looked up the results of this race over the past five years. He checked the condition of the track in past years, something he rarely did. He researched the records of the horses. He reviewed their pedigrees. He looked up each jockey's record this year. He immersed himself in every aspect of the race. The hours he spent doing this almost equaled the hours he was putting in to the merger problem.

———

Kevin had not noticed the significance of his great withdrawal to problem-solving mode when he was faced with the threat of losing his department, and having to share control of his future. He likewise didn't recognize the significance of his problem-solving obsession about the outcome of the race. Just as before, if he had recognized that he was doing "his thing"—that he was repeating his usual defensive style when faced with anxiety—he might have seen his intense focus on the race as a signpost. He might have realized that he was trying to manage a great deal of anxiety. It was anxiety about the same things that were bothering him before he saw the article in the paper. Many races are hard to call in advance. There was no unusual opportunity in this race. Kevin was just heading toward his addiction.

Clearly, while Kevin was obsessed with figuring out the race, he was already on the road to his addictive act. The key moment in his addictive process was when he first sighted the article in the paper and started to ponder what to do. If he was pondering, he was already on his way. He would have been able to see that for himself if, when he read the article, he had simply started to think about where to place his bets.

But his defensive style prevented him from seeing the key moment for what it was. Instead of thinking, "I'm going to bet on this race," he turned the race into a challenge to solve. There were certain factors in this race that made it special, he told himself. It was just the kind of thing he could figure out, he thought.

By creating an intellectual problem he could solve, Kevin overlooked the feelings that were actually driving him. His defensive style kept him from recognizing that he was being driven toward his addiction.

Karen

Karen was a compulsive eater. She was overweight because of it, and she hated that. It seemed like she had been dealing with eating and weight for nearly all of her twenty-seven years. Of course, she had tried countless diets. She read every new idea in the magazines she bought each month (and there was a supposedly new idea in almost every issue). She had been to support groups, bought food programs, and tried various diet pills all "guaranteed to help you lose weight." Like many people, she had in fact lost weight many times, only to quickly regain it. The cycle was disillusioning and depressing. Even though she kept trying, inside she doubted she would ever be able to control her eating.

If you saw Karen in a restaurant you would wonder why she was so overweight. Most of the time she ordered salads and a diet soft drink. But when she was home it was a different story. Though she tried her best, she could not keep from bingeing. She often went through a quart of ice cream or a full jar of peanut butter or a bag of cookies in a sitting. Potato chips and cake were regular items. If there were leftovers they were often gone by morning. A big bowl of leftover pasta followed by ice cream was a bedtime snack.

Karen did not binge all the time, however. The fact that she felt awful—physically and emotionally—after a binge was one factor. But more deeply, she did not always have the intense drive toward her addiction any more than people with alcoholism have the same drive to drink every day. So there were good days and bad, depending on what was going on inside her mind. But since she didn't know about these deeper factors, the timing of her binges seemed as random and confusing to her as why she had them.

Karen was married and worked part-time as a substitute teacher. Her husband, Larry, was an accountant at a medium-size accounting firm. The couple had one child, an eighteen-month-old little boy named Sam. She and Larry had been having intense talks about whether to put Sam in a day-care program so Karen could go back to school part-time. It was a dilemma, since the reason Karen was working at all was to bring in some extra money. Her return to school would be expensive and would also mean the added cost of day care for Sam. The only reason her substitute teaching was possible was because they had close friends who would watch the baby when Karen was called in to work. But they could not be expected to take care of Sam every day. Longer term, of course, the idea was for Karen to be able to make more money. But getting from where they were to that endpoint felt like jumping over the Grand Canyon.

Karen had always wanted to be a teacher. Later, when she became an American history major in college and loved her subject, she knew that teaching it to college students was what she wanted to do. But to teach at that level she had to have a graduate degree. The substitute teaching in elementary schools that she was doing now was okay—at least she was teaching—but it was not her dream.

Karen and Larry were aware of this eventual problem even before they were married, and they thought they had solved it. They both had plans for careers, and they both wanted to have a child. Their idea was to do just what they did. Karen would stay home with the baby for a year or two and then return to school part-time. This seemed reasonable at the time because they imagined Larry would make a good deal more money than he did. But when the economy stagnated, Larry's starting salary was lower than they had expected, and it did not go up. Actually, he was fortunate to have a decent job at all. Karen's dreams for her career were stuck on hold. She had good reasons to be depressed and worried.

Throughout her life Karen had eaten food when she had those feelings. But she generally didn't think about heading toward a binge until she was staring in the refrigerator or at the shelf where the cookies lived. She usually had an internal struggle at those moments about whether or not to eat. Sometimes she was able to have a bit more control. But mostly she could not stop herself from eating because by the time she was gazing at the food it was too late, as with all other addictive acts. And as with other forms of addiction, it would have been very helpful for her to be able to recognize the key moment on the path toward a binge, long before it was right in front of her.

But picking up on those earliest moments was especially hard for her because of her brand of defense. Not only was she unaware that she was using a defense, but her particular defense interfered with her thinking itself.

One example had occurred a couple of months earlier. Karen had gone to her doctor for a routine checkup. Her doctor had asked her to have lab tests run before the visit so she could review them with Karen when they met. When she came home from the visit, Larry asked her how it went.

KAREN: Oh, I don't know. It was fine I guess.

LARRY: What do you mean, "you guess"?

KAREN: She said I have some sort of sugar thing.

LARRY: What "sugar thing"?

KAREN: Something in the lab results. It's probably nothing.

LARRY: What results? Come on, what aren't you telling me?

KAREN: Nothing, really. It's just some abnormal test. I guess she'll do it over.

LARRY: What test? And what do you mean you guess she'll do it over? Is she going to do it over?

KAREN: Yes, she wants me to come back for another level after I haven't eaten overnight.

LARRY: So she *is* going to do it over. It was a blood sugar level?

KAREN: Yes.

LARRY: What else did she say?

KAREN: I don't know. She was just talking about the levels and what level means a problem and what level means it *could* be a problem but isn't really a problem. I just can't explain it all.

LARRY: But you understood it? I mean, when she told you?

KAREN: Well, maybe, not really.

LARRY (*finally becoming exasperated*): So, why didn't you ask her to explain it better?

KAREN: I just didn't care. She'll redo the test and she'll decide what to do from there.

Karen's reaction to the abnormal blood test sounded like she really didn't care. And it was true that Karen was not an alarmist about medical issues. But in this case she was worried. Her mother and an aunt had diabetes, and she was overweight. She had been nervous about her blood sugars when she was pregnant, and had been very relieved that they had stayed within the normal range for a pregnant woman. But since childhood she had harbored a deep fear of being sick and dying from diabetes. And from an early age, she had dealt with her sense of dread by eating.

So this particular medical issue worried her, and that evening she had trouble sleeping because of it.

What did it mean, then, that Karen didn't appear to have paid close attention to what the doctor told her? Why was she so confused and confusing when she talked about it?

Being confused (and therefore, confusing) was a main defense that Karen had developed for dealing with her anxiety. If she was mixed up, didn't understand things, or couldn't clearly think about them, then she didn't have to know them. It was an elegant system in its own way. If you can't grasp ideas that would make you anxious or sad, then you don't have to feel anxious or sad.

Of course, this defensive style had its drawbacks. She kept herself from knowing things it would have been important for her to know. Being confused also risked others becoming annoyed with her, as in the example above. But Karen was mostly oblivious to the frustration she caused others. It wasn't that she didn't care, but rather that she didn't see that she was *doing* anything. It was just so hard to keep track of things, she told herself.

Her defensive style now interfered with her locating the earliest moment on her path to a binge. Since she could not sleep, Karen got out of bed and sat at the kitchen table devouring a box of chocolate cookies.

Now, several months after the incident with the lab tests, Karen and Larry decided that it made sense for her to talk with someone at a graduate school in which she was interested, to get a feel for the process and her chances of being admitted. She arranged to speak with Harold Campbell, a prominent professor in the Department of History. They met in his office first thing in the morning.

KAREN: I've been out of the field for almost five years, but I'm excited to return. I'm hoping to be able to teach in college.

CAMPBELL: Five years is a long time.

KAREN: Well, we got married, had a child. He's a year-and-a-half now and we're thinking that this is a good time for me to go back to school.

CAMPBELL: Yes, I see. Most of our students begin our graduate program directly from college, which creates a continuity that is useful for studying a specialty area. The more a student retains from his or her general history background, the better prepared she is to consider the narrower area of her study in graduate school.

KAREN: Well, yes, that makes sense. I've been keeping

my hand in, though. I've been working part-time as a substitute teacher.

CAMPBELL: Where do you do that?

KAREN: It's our local elementary school. I substitute in all grades, K through six.

CAMPBELL: Oh. I thought you meant in history. You teach small children.

KAREN: Well, yes. But I feel it keeps my teaching skills up. I love to teach.

CAMPBELL (*after a pause*): I see. (*Another pause.*) So, teaching history is your main goal?

KAREN: Yes, I've wanted to be a college history teacher ever since I took my first history class in college, I think.

CAMPBELL: You're not interested in research?

KAREN (*taken aback*): Um, no, not particularly.

CAMPBELL: Well, you know we try to turn out people who will advance the field. If you want to eventually be a history professor at a place like this you will need to publish academic papers. To do that you will need to do research. I've found that our graduate students who go on to do best have a natural interest in research.

KAREN: Well, I . . . I guess my main interest is in teaching. Couldn't the school consider someone for graduate study who is interested in that?

CAMPBELL: We expect all our students to be able to teach. Frankly, we are looking for more than that.

KAREN: I . . . I thought . . . well, okay. Thank you for your time speaking with me today.

CAMPBELL: Thank you for coming in to see me.

When she left the office Karen felt confused. What did Professor Campbell really say? He seemed to like research, but he said he expected his students to teach. She had been away from school for five years, but did that matter? He said he understood that, didn't he? Did he think her substitute-teacher work was a good thing or not? Karen shook her head. It was hard to make out what to do with what she found out in that interview.

She returned home. Larry had been watching the baby but now had to go in to work. He asked how it went. Karen shrugged her shoulders. "It was okay, I guess." Larry had to run out the door. "Okay," he said, "I'll talk to you later."

Sam was sleepy, and Karen soon put him down for a nap. She needed to get some laundry done and they needed more diapers at the store. It was almost time for lunch. She looked in the refrigerator. Maybe she would just have a sandwich. There was also a bowl of leftover chicken and rice from last night. It was enough for tonight's dinner. Karen looked at the bowl. "I shouldn't eat it," she thought. She took it out and put it in the microwave. An hour later she had eaten all of it, then took out a Fudgsicle from her freezer and ate that too.

Afterward, she felt awful. "Why do I do this?" she said to herself. "There really is no reason at all."

We can see that Karen's binge eating was precipitated by her depressing interview with Professor Campbell. She had felt attacked, devalued, and finally despondent about her chances at the school. Her anxiety about her career plans was far higher after the interview than before. This all could have been a clear sign to her that she was at risk of repeating her addictive behavior. But she didn't see it. Her feelings during and after her meeting with Professor Campbell were a jumble in her mind. She wasn't even sure there was a problem. She was unprepared for her addictive act that soon followed.

As with the other people we've seen, if Karen had known that becoming confused was her way to deal with upsetting feelings she could have stood apart from her defense and seen it for what it was. If she was getting confused, she must be more upset than she knew. Recognizing this, she could have sat down and thought about what was so upsetting. And even if she still couldn't stay with her feelings, because they were too frightening, she could at least have recognized that her level of confusion meant trouble. She could have realized that she was at high risk for a binge and taken some action to prevent it before it became overwhelming.

———

Getting to know the defensive styles you use when faced with something uncomfortable can be extremely helpful in catching the key moment in your addiction. If you cast your mind back through your life you can probably notice the main ones. Do you try to push thoughts out of mind, like Marjorie? Do you try to out-tough problems rather than look into them, like Brian? Do you try to rationalize your problems away, like Steven? Do you turn emotions into intellectual problems to solve, like Kevin, or become unclear in your thinking when you are upset, like Karen? There are innumerable other ways to deal with uncomfortable issues. As you read about different people in the rest of this book, try to notice what defensive styles they use. It's good practice for noticing your own style. Besides helping to pick up your addictive process earlier, knowing how you work emotionally is good for living in general.

You will find that seeing your defenses for what they are is a bit like opening the door to a room. Inside, concealed behind the defenses, will be the emotional issues that are the most important to you in your life. Needless to say, if you have an addiction, these are also the issues that lie behind your addiction. We will look at these issues in the next two chapters.

First, now that we've looked at ways you may conceal the key moment in your addiction, let's return to that moment and take a closer look at what is happening there.

STEP 5

Understanding What Is Happening at the Key Moment in Addiction

We've seen that it doesn't make sense to spend time looking at the effects of addictive acts, and it isn't much more useful to spend energy focusing on addictive acts themselves. We know that the key moment in an addictive process is always earlier, and sometimes much earlier than when you actually do your addictive act. We also know that the key moment can be hard to find, and that you may even defensively conceal it from yourself.

In that key moment are the factors that cause addiction. If it is possible to understand what is happening then, that means your addiction can be understood, and ultimately mastered.

Each of the people whose stories we've considered had strong feelings in those critical moments, though the issues were different for different people. Let's take a look at another person and see if we can use his story to better understand what goes on in these key moments.

DANIEL

Daniel's childhood seemed the sort people would make pleasant G-rated movies about. His father was a doctor with a successful practice, his mother was a devoted wife and mother who was happy making a home for her family, and his brother, Arthur—two and a half years older than Daniel—was a handsome, athletic, popular guy with lots of friends. Daniel himself was a quiet, obedient boy. He was smart and good in school and would eventually go on to become a doctor like his dad. Viewing this G-rated family from the outside, one would wonder why Daniel later developed such severe alcoholism that he eventually lost his health, his marriage, and his ability to practice his profession.

Within the walls of his house, Daniel was desperately unhappy. His mother spanked him for getting dirty from playing outside. His older brother regularly "playfully" wrestled him into submission, despite his tears and cries of protest. His father enjoyed watching the boys wrestle, seeing it as normal high jinks, and ignored Daniel's pleas for help. As he grew up, Daniel remained quiet and obedient. What choice did he have? His brother, enmeshed in his own needs to dominate his younger brother, would have responded to Daniel's asserting himself by beating him more. His father would have considered him weak had he complained. His mother was set on Daniel being just the way he was: the neat, compliant boy she had hoped her first son would be— before he was overtaken by her husband's need to make sure he was an alpha male. (It was Daniel's father's dedication to seeing Arthur as a powerful man that blinded him to Daniel's suffering at Arthur's hands.)

Daniel was forty years old and still working as a physician in a local emergency room when he ran into trouble with a contractor he had hired to rebuild his old wooden garage, which was almost falling down. The contractor had started the project and then left in the middle, after Daniel had paid him in advance nearly the entire cost of the job. After several calls from Daniel the contractor finally called back, saying he could not finish the garage now because he had started another job. It would be at least three weeks before he could get back to it.

Daniel protested, but weakly. He told the contractor that he wasn't being fair. He reminded the contractor that he had been paid in advance because the contractor had insisted on that before starting, and now he wasn't fulfilling his side of the bargain. He said he was living with the mess that was next to his house where the garage was half-built. He said that he had a garage to keep his car out of the weather, and now it was sitting outside. In response to all this, the contractor said there was nothing he could do. Daniel would just have to wait.

It had been almost a week since Daniel had had a drink, which made this week one of his longer periods of abstinence. But after this conversation, he was drinking within a half hour, or as long as it took for him to get to the liquor store and return.

The telephone call is pretty clearly the key moment in this episode of Daniel's drinking, though one could say that the pressure had been building ever since he began making phone calls without hearing back from the contractor. Daniel was perfectly aware of this himself. But what was happening in that moment? If you had asked him, he would have said that he was frustrated. That was true, of course. But let's say you were his friend and you pressed him further about that moment. The conversation might have gone like this:

> You: I can see why you were upset. But what do you think really frustrated you?
>
> Daniel: I was planning on having the garage done. Now I'm going to have to wait three weeks with the mess in the driveway and my car on the street.

You: And the way the contractor is dealing with you, I
  suppose.

DANIEL: Yes, of course.

You: So, it's not just the garage itself. It's the whole situation.

DANIEL: Yes.

You: I wonder how important the garage part of this is.

DANIEL: What do you mean? It's the garage that's the
  problem.

You: Well, what if it rained for three weeks? If the contractor
  called each day to say he couldn't work on the garage that
  day because of the rain, would you be just as frustrated?

DANIEL: I wouldn't be happy about the delay. But I guess the
  answer is no. If the delay was because of the rain, no, it
  wouldn't bother me as much.

You: How come?

DANIEL: Rain is nobody's fault. I can't get too angry about it.

You: So, the garage part, the problem of having to wait for
  the garage to be done, doesn't sound like the main thing
  frustrating you. You're more bothered by the trouble with
  the contractor.

DANIEL: Well, when you put it that way, I guess so. What
  difference does it make?

You: I assumed that you drank because you were frustrated.

DANIEL: Yes, obviously.

You: Well, that's why it's important. You didn't drink because
  the garage wasn't getting done. You drank because of the
  way the contractor treated you.

DANIEL: Fine. Who cares?

You: If we can eliminate the garage part we can focus better
  on what really triggered your drinking.

DANIEL: But I already know what that is. He's screwing me.
  He took the money then he went off to do another job.
  Anybody would be frustrated.

You: Sure, but you were very, very frustrated. You're trying
     not to drink yet you said that it took no time at all before
     you were off to the liquor store. Probably if you had a
     drink handy you would have been drinking it the instant
     you got off the phone.

Daniel: I'm sure I would.

You: And here's another thing. Remember last month
     when you told me about waiting on a line to get into a
     restaurant? You were frustrated then, too, when someone
     behind you got taken first. But you didn't drink.

Daniel: That was different. You're forgetting that I went
     to the maître d' and told him what happened and I was
     seated immediately.

You: So, what was different?

Daniel: I could do something about it, then. Here I'm stuck.
     He has my money already.

You: Exactly. The difference here is that you're stuck. I'm
     thinking that being stuck puts the frustration on a whole
     different level.

Daniel (*after a pause*): Maybe you're right. (*Another pause.*)
     Maybe being stuck puts things on the level that I drink.

What was happening in the key moment of Daniel's addiction
was not just about the real-life problem of a half-finished garage.
It was about the feelings evoked in him by the conversation with
the contractor. Moreover, it was not just about feeling that he was
being screwed. It was about feeling stuck. Unlike the situation at
the restaurant, here he felt helpless to do anything about it.

It is not hard to see that Daniel's weak reaction to the contractor was a reflection of his early life. He had always felt he had to
put up with being beaten, both literally by his brother and beaten
down by the demands of both his parents, and his solution had
been to be obedient as a child, continuing this adaptation later as a

meek adult. When the contractor took advantage of him, he was emotionally back in the old situation of his childhood. That had been a trap, and he experienced this as another trap.

His answer to his life of frustrating traps was an addiction. Maybe he was helpless to deal with the contractor, but he could do *something*. He could drink. When he drank he took charge of his emotional life. He could change the way he felt by performing an act that he knew would make him feel better, and that was entirely in his control. No contractor, or brother or father or mother for that matter, was going to crush him, making him be a good boy.

What was happening in Daniel's key moment was that he felt helpless. Of course the details of this—what made him as an individual feel so helpless—would ultimately be essential for him to know in order to master his addiction, and we will look at that later in the book. But for now, the main point is this:

The feeling at the key moment along the path to addictive behavior is helplessness or powerlessness. It feels like you are in a trap that you can do nothing about.

Let's look at another example:

MATTHEW

You could hardly find someone less like Daniel (in the example above) than Matthew R. Gallagher. Far from being meek, Matthew projected power. He was a corporate attorney in charge of his division within a firm that employed hundreds of lawyers with branch offices in five states. When he entered a room he expected to be treated like the important person he knew he was, and that was just how he was treated, especially among the lawyers and assistants at the firm.

Despite his considerable success, Matthew was an addictive cocaine user. In his earlier days he believed that cocaine helped him in his work. He felt energized, needed less sleep (at least until he crashed), and thought his ideas were more brilliant than usual. The fact was that Matthew's cocaine use led him to come up with ideas that seemed brilliant only while he was high on cocaine. The next day they regularly needed to be revised or scrapped. The drug also interfered with his sleep, which made him irritable and interfered with his concentration the next day. However, even at less than his best, Matthew really was brilliant at his work and the cocaine didn't interfere enough to keep him from moving up the partnership ladder at his firm.

Over the years, though, he had come to see that the drug was a problem. He was never able to stop completely, but he had cut down substantially, which pleased him. But that changed the night he not only smoked cocaine again, but also stayed up all night to do so and missed a morning meeting with one of the firm's most important clients as a result. He had not used the drug all night for many years.

The day before, Matthew had been consulted by one of his junior partners about how to deal with a tricky problem with another client. This client was not quite as large as the one whose meeting Matthew would miss the next day, but it was still a significant part of the firm's practice. When the partner came in, it was clear to Matthew that his question was more about human relations than the law. The partner explained that the CEO and major owner of a company the firm represented was angry about the firm's slow response to his request. The CEO had asked that the firm file suit against one of the client's competitors, and the firm had not done so. The partner explained that this had been intentional because the firm's lawyers did not believe their client had a winnable case. They had been trying, therefore, to talk him out of pursuing it. Filing cases that would be thrown out because they were considered frivolous was not good for either the client or the law firm. But the CEO had ignored the firm's advice and was now increasingly impatient with them.

That day, matters had come to a head. The client had threatened to leave the firm to seek legal help from one of the other giant firms in the city, taking with him a large chunk of business. That quickly brought the junior partner into Matthew's office.

When he heard the story, Matthew had been reassuring. He told the partner to have the client come in for a meeting the next day and that Matthew himself would attend, to calm the waters. The junior partner nodded and left the office with his marching orders.

But later that afternoon the partner was back in Matthew's office. He had bad news. He had followed Matthew's advice and the client had blown up. "It's just more delay!" the client had shouted into the phone. No matter how much the partner had attempted to soothe him, the client had just become angrier. The conversation ended with the CEO saying, "You're fired. My new attorneys will be in touch with you to obtain the company records I sent you." Then he hung up.

Matthew was taken aback. He pointedly asked his junior partner how he had begun the conversation. Was he too abrupt, did he fail to give the client a chance to air his views, did he tell him that Matthew himself would be at the new meeting? No, no, yes. The partner had been appropriate, professional, and courteous. Matthew then began to think out loud about whether it made more sense to call the client back today or write him a letter. As he thought this over, he told the junior partner that this reaction by a client was highly unusual at the firm, something he had rarely seen in his many years of experience in these matters. Matthew shook his head in agitation.

Finally, he declared that the problem was that the client was an idiot. He told the partner that he, Matthew, would call the client later in the day and try to patch things up.

Matthew did call an hour later, after he had calmed somewhat. But that had gone badly, too. The client refused to speak with him, even leaving a message through his secretary that if Matthew wanted to discuss arrangements for the transfer of the client's records to the new law firm, he could speak with an assistant.

That was what happened the day of Matthew's cocaine binge. So, when was the key moment? It must have been sometime during that day, hours before he began using cocaine that evening. In the first meeting with his junior partner, when Matthew learned that the client was angry, he hadn't seemed upset at all. In fact, he was calm and reassuring to his colleague. Of course, we know from the discussion in Step 4 that this could have been a defense. Maybe Matthew was more disturbed about the news than he let on, or even than he knew himself. In that case, the key moment for him could have been during that first meeting. So, we have to keep that possibility in mind until we know better what was going on in Matthew's mind that triggered his addictive act. Certainly the second meeting with the junior partner, when Matthew was startled and upset by the news that his advice had backfired, is a strong candidate for the key moment.

But what was happening in that moment? To answer this, we have to know what about this situation was so emotionally important to Matthew that it could set off his addictive response.

Matthew grew up in an apartment house in a large city until the family moved to a house in the suburbs when he was six. His father was an immigrant to the United States who lived the American success story. Arriving in this country with very little, he had built a small clothing store into a chain of retail stores that sold clothes, accessories, cosmetics, and more. The family's move to a house had followed the opening of Mr. Gallagher's third store. But Matthew's father never really felt proud of himself. Because he had never graduated from high school, he considered himself an "uneducated man." That would never be said about his children, he swore to himself. As things turned out, this determination would apply first to Matthew, then three years later to his sister, Kathleen.

Both of Matthew's parents were deeply concerned with their children's success, but for his father it meant something deeper— and it showed. Mr. Gallagher insisted that the children, and particularly Matthew, be perfect in their studies from the earliest grades. When his father felt Matthew wasn't being challenged enough at school he brought in tutors to supplement his schoolwork. "Work at it until you get it right," his father told him a thousand times as he walked by the boy working with his tutor. His father's advice expressed both his educational dreams for his son and his own demanding work ethic that had helped him build a small clothing empire from almost nothing. Later, as Matthew grew old enough to have graded tests in school, he learned that bringing home a score of 96 meant having to explain which question he got wrong.

Matthew might have come out of all this with only intense feelings about getting his schoolwork right. But there was more to his father's message and Matthew heard it. He could feel in his bones that getting things right, to his father, meant much more than learning things. Getting things right was about self-respect.

This was something with which Mr. Gallagher had struggled his entire life. With a loving family, devoted children, and his success at his work, he ought to have felt wonderful about himself. But he didn't, for reasons having to do with his own past. After he grew up and came to the United States, his self-doubt became centered on the one thing in his new country that he was convinced kept him from being fully respected: his lack of formal education. Later, his self-doubt transformed into his fierce determination that his children not only be educated, but also be at the top of their class.

Not only did Matthew go to college, but he also followed that by attending one of the most prestigious law schools in the country before moving on to the prestigious law firm where he had now risen to be head of a division. He had done it all through the same hard work ethic as his father. Combined with his outstanding intellect, this meant that when it came to his field he was very nearly always right.

But as you can imagine, there was a downside to all this. Always being right wasn't the problem. The problem was that he *had* to always be right—because what was at stake was self-respect. That meant that if he was ever wrong, he felt ashamed. Throughout his life Matthew lived with the same vulnerability to feeling shame that his father had lived with. It was a sad irony that while his father had tried his hardest to prevent his children from the self-doubt with which he lived, in his intensity to have them get everything right he had created the same problem in them. He had conveyed the very belief from which he suffered—that it was desperately important to get things right because otherwise you aren't worth much.

Matthew's reaction to being wrong about his client now makes more sense. As usual with addictions (and psychological symptoms in general) the issue was not what was on the surface but the personal meaning that lay beneath. The key moment in Matthew's addictive path was the second meeting with the junior partner, when Matthew was confronted with being wrong. In the first meeting, Matthew believed he had solved the problem; he was still the man with the right answers. But in the second meeting, he could not avoid seeing that he was wrong, and wrong in a way that was both significant for the firm and would be known by many. This wasn't a private decision; it was advice to a subordinate. In Matthew's mind, his shame was public.

Matthew's reaction was to try to shrug off this shameful responsibility. He questioned his partner about whether the partner had approached the client incorrectly. He made a point of saying how unusual it was for a client to react this way, which meant that it would be unfair to lose regard for Matthew because of the client's reaction. Finally, he tried to place all of the blame on the client: he was an idiot.

These maneuvers only helped to forestall Matthew's problem. An hour later, when he tried to reach the client himself and was unsuccessful, he was finally trapped. Faced with his helplessness over the shame he had battled his whole life, he could not stand still and he did not. His furious, repetitive use of cocaine for the entire night expressed his rage at the helplessness that was so awful for him.

———

The story of Matthew's life and the areas where he felt the most vulnerable were quite different from Daniel and his life. Everyone is different. But what links everybody together is the feeling of helplessness that overwhelms them in the key moments of their addiction.

Knowing this provides another tool for both finding and identifying the key moment in your own addictive path. If you can learn to recognize that sensation of being trapped, that feeling of hopelessness and helplessness, then you have the chance to stop and scrutinize what is going on in your life and in your mind before you get close to acting on your addiction. Even if you are not aware that you are under stress, even if you are completely unaware of the main emotional issues that cause problems for you in your life, as long as you can pick up on your feeling of helplessness you have a chance to catch your addiction early. At that point you can think about your situation, and about whether it is the kind of position that in the past has led you toward your addiction. If you can do this, you will be turning the tables on your addiction. You will be making use of the central emotion of addictive behavior—the feeling of being trapped and helpless—as an ally. You will be turning it into a siren that warns you that the key moment on the path to addiction has arrived. And as we know, if you can catch the key moment in your addiction, you will know that your addictive act is around the corner.

There is one more advantage to recognizing the feeling of helplessness. Everyone is different, but all you have to know are the central issues that lead *you* to feel intolerably helpless. Recognizing what kinds of things cause you to feel overwhelmingly helpless is like having a giant arrow pointing to the central issues behind your addiction, which will always also be the central issues that give you trouble in your life. We will return to look at exactly those issues when we come to the final step in breaking your addiction in Step 7.

But first let's look at what you can do in the short term, when your addiction is upon you.

STEP 6

Short-Term Strategies for Dealing with Addiction

We've seen how addictions work. We know that if you can locate the key moment when the drive toward an addiction starts, you will be in a good position to do something about it—before the feeling becomes overwhelming. We've looked at how to identify that key moment. We also identified ways you can sometimes keep this moment hidden from your own view. We know that in that key moment there is a sense of helplessness or powerlessness, a feeling of being in a trap. Now, in Step 6, we will examine strategies for escaping the helplessness trap.

Let's begin by looking at an example that we already know from Step 3 and Step 4: the story of Marjorie. Marjorie took her pills after throwing a weekend party that she did not want to have. We learned that the key moment in the path to her addictive behavior was not the day she took the pills, but days before, when she sat at the kitchen table planning her shopping for the upcoming weekend and had the first fleeting thoughts of using her drugs. We also saw that she had a defense that kept her from seeing this key moment: when she was faced with uncomfortable thoughts, she regularly pushed them out of mind. Having done this, she didn't have to feel uncomfortable for the moment, but the cost was being unaware of what she thought or felt. As a result, she didn't recognize her key moment and lost the chance to stop the march toward her addiction.

If Marjorie had realized the importance of that moment she could have considered whether there was anything else she could do to counter her feelings of helplessness, instead of taking drugs. Actually there was a very long list of possible actions that would have made her feel less helpless. She could have asked her guests to bring their own potluck food, or even arranged to have some- one else cater her party. Or she could have arranged for her guests to stay somewhere other than her home while they were visiting, or made the visit shorter, or canceled the party altogether. Or, as long as she was aware of what was going on emotionally within her, she could have chosen to just go ahead with the weekend but made sure that she was not going to play her usual role of half- host, half-servant.

None of these possibilities crossed Marjorie's mind because when she first had the thought of taking her pills she ignored it. But let's say she had learned that pushing thoughts out of mind was one of her main defenses, as we talked about in Step 4. Once she acknowledged to herself that she was think- ing about taking pills, she would have been in the position to ask herself *why* that was the case. She would have recognized right away that she was feeling trapped and helpless. Certainly at that point she would have immediately realized what she felt helpless about: it was the weekend party that she was planning at that very moment. At this point in her thinking she would have been almost home free. Once she recognized that her sense of being duty-bound to throw the party was the source of her helpless feelings, then the many possible solutions to this problem would have become clear. After all, the possible solutions, such as having guests bring their own food or shortening the weekend, are pretty obvious once you know what the problem is.

What makes solutions to addiction-triggering situations so easy to find? The answer is in the nature of addiction. When people feel that they cannot act directly against helplessness (usually because it would make them feel too guilty or anxious) they resort to a displaced action—the addictive behavior. Consequently, in searching for alternatives when you are faced with your addiction, what you are really doing is simply undoing that displacement.

The solutions to the helplessness traps that lead to addiction are just the direct actions that would have automatically come to mind if there were not some emotional factor preventing you from acting directly.

"How can this be so easy?" you may ask. The truth is, it isn't. Acting on more direct alternative behaviors at the moment you are overcome with a sense of helplessness can be as difficult as it is essential. After all, your mind seeks out a substitute behavior (the addiction itself) at this key moment because it does not see—or does not want to see—other alternatives. In Marjorie's case, her lifelong problem with knowing and expressing her feelings had kept her from thinking directly about ways to get out of throwing a party for her relatives. So it wasn't easy for her to reverse the displacement and reconsider taking a direct action to deal with her trap.

What can you do to break out of your helplessness trap? As I said at the close of Step 5, there are two paths from here. In the longer term, someone like Marjorie can work out the deeper causes of her feeling obliged to serve others and her fear of doing things for herself. If she could do this, it would be the best guarantee that she could stay away from her addiction in the future. I will return to this in the next chapter.

But another short-term strategy allows you to master your addiction *now* in just the way I've described, without having all the underlying issues worked out yet. If Marjorie had gone through the steps I described—identifying the key moment, recognizing the source of her feelings of helplessness at that moment, and then seeing the array of alternative actions open to her—she would have improved her chances of avoiding her old "solution" of using pills days later. In the short term, she didn't have to address the complex emotions underlying her sense of helplessness in situations like these; she only needed to find a way to deal with this one situation right now. And that was a much more manageable task.

When seeking alternatives to addictive behavior, you don't need to come up with the best possible alternative. You only need to come up with an action that addresses your predicament more directly than the addictive act.

In Marjorie's case, she may not have been able to cancel the party because it would have made her too anxious, even though that was what she really most wanted to do. She might not have been able to bring herself to shorten the stay of her guests either. But even if she had just scaled back her plans, knowing that she had to do something to deal with her helplessness, it very likely would have been sufficient to keep her from taking pills. The reason this works is that the "helplessness trap" at the heart of addiction can be relieved by almost any action that restores some sense of power, thereby reducing the pressure to repeat an addictive act.

Let's look at some different kinds of addiction-inducing situations and how they can be dealt with using short-term strategies.

ERIC

At thirty-five years old, Eric had long thought of himself as a "functional alcoholic." He meant that even though he drank too much, he had a family, friends, a steady job in a small law firm, and good health. His drinking was almost entirely in brief binges and he was okay between them, so it was easy for him to minimize the effects of his drinking. The binges were a problem, though. As much as his wife loved him, there had been gradually increasing tension between them as his drinking continued over the years. And there was also another big problem. He had been arrested twice for driving under the influence, and both times he had lost his license as a result. The arrests also caused him embarrassment (personal and professional) and put more strain on his marriage. Still, it wasn't until the second arrest that Eric's mild view of his drinking was shaken. He had driven off the road and nearly rolled his car when the wheels near the curbside of the road dropped into a ditch. He realized that he could have killed himself or someone else. That was when he began to think in earnest about stopping his drinking altogether.

He felt this wouldn't be too hard, for the same reasons he had been able to minimize his drinking. He had always thought of his drinking as something he did to "relax" when he was tense or upset. If this was why he drank, then surely it wouldn't be too hard to quit. All he needed to do was find another way to relax. He had no idea that his drinking was connected to deeper issues, that he was relying on it as a temporary solution for situations in which he felt intolerably helpless. Consequently, when he found himself drinking again soon after deciding to quit for good, he was both confused and worried.

It was one evening after a late meeting at his law firm. He had attended a gathering of about fifteen colleagues to talk about plans for the firm's future. They needed to decide about moving to a larger space or even buying a small building to house them. At the same time, their growth meant that there were questions about procedures to add new partners, and financial issues associated with that. The discussion was spirited, almost heated, since some of the firm's members felt very strongly about keeping the firm basically as it was while others felt equally strongly about expanding, which would require the move to new quarters and major changes in the way they ran the company.

Eric sat silently throughout the meeting. It wasn't that he didn't have an opinion or didn't care. He had talked with a few of his colleagues who agreed with him about the need to expand, and he felt as strongly as anyone in the room. But every time he almost spoke up he held himself back. He wasn't a very senior member. Thoughts came to his mind but he questioned them. Maybe he would sound foolish. There were strong feelings in the room, and one of the more senior people who disagreed with him might cut him down. Each time he was about to speak he hesitated, and the moment was lost.

Finally the meeting was over. Nothing had been resolved, and small groups of people were standing around talking about various aspects of the issues, either with allies or in continued argument with those on the other side. Eric glanced around, but didn't feel comfortable joining any of these impromptu groups. He put on his coat and left by himself.

When he arrived home his wife and their two kids had already eaten. Eric wasn't hungry anyway. He told his wife he'd had a tough day and needed some peace. He went into his small home office and took the bottle of whiskey from his desk drawer and began to drink.

———

After this episode, Eric sought some help, which was how I came to know him. As we talked about his addiction and his life he came to recognize the emotional factors underlying his urge to drink, and how his drinking was a way to manage these factors. We learned that Eric had been anxious in competitive situations his whole life. His withdrawal during that last company meeting was typical for him. It wasn't so much that he was filled with self-doubt. He knew he could figure out the issues being discussed. Telling himself that he wasn't sure what to say was actually a de-fense—a reason he gave himself for why he didn't speak up. More deeply, he lived with a great fear of challenging others, especially parent-like figures like the more senior, older members of his firm. What if he antagonized them and they reacted violently? When he was small, that was the sort of thing that terrified him. In fact, when he thought during the meeting that one of them might "cut him down" he was inadvertently thinking in exactly the terms he had feared as a child.

It was because Eric inhibited himself in these competitive situations that he ended up feeling so helpless. At the meeting he had felt humiliated by his silence, and his rage at this old humiliating helplessness propelled him into his usual displaced action. When he returned home, he drank for three hours before falling asleep at the desk in his home office.

But now that Eric was seeing the way his addiction worked, he had the same tools available to him that you have from read-ing this far. As it turned out, the chance to put these tools to use would come soon.

It was a clear-blue-sky day, perfect to go to a baseball game. Eric and three of his friends—Greg, Andy, and Keith—had bought tickets to the game and they had each driven there in time for the national anthem. They had good seats down the right field sideline, just past first base. Eric was a true fan of the game. There was no doubting his passion for the home team, but he also loved the intricacies of the sport. Because he had played baseball in high school he watched with more awareness than the casual fan. He looked at changes in placement of the fielders according to who was pitching, the pitch count, and of course, who was at bat and the game situation. He watched the way the pitcher and catcher chose to deal with different batters and did his best to tell the pattern of pitches that were being thrown, although the truth was that he could tell this better on TV than from where he was sitting.

By the sixth inning things were going badly for his team. They were losing 9 to 2. Hope of a comeback depended in large part on the ability of the team's relief pitchers to hold down the visitors while hoping the home team could rally. Unfortunately, the relief pitching on Eric's team was a chronic source of despair for the team's fans. Two of the team's relievers had already been brought in to pitch in this game and both were quickly sent to the showers after a hail of opponents' line drive hits. Meanwhile, the starting pitcher for the opposition seemed to be getting stronger as the game progressed. After Eric's team went down in order in the bottom of the sixth inning, many of the fans began to leave.

"What do you say, guys?" Greg said.

"It's not looking too good. That's what I say," Andy answered with a laugh. Keith just shook his head.

"So, want to go?" Greg asked.

"Yeah, let's get out of here," Keith said.

Andy added, "It's okay with me. I've absorbed enough torture for one day."

"Eric?" Greg said, turning to him.

Eric sat a moment. He didn't really care that the game was lopsided and a likely loss for his team. He wanted to stay. He had come to see baseball. But everyone else wanted to go, and he didn't want to be the drag on the group. He just shrugged.

Greg looked at him. "What? You don't want to go?"

Keith said, "C'mon Eric. This game is over."

Andy added, "Yeah. We're toast, man."

Eric hesitated again. Almost simultaneously he had two thoughts. First, he thought, "Okay, I'll leave with them," followed instantly by the thought, "I'll have a drink when I get home."

At this point, Eric recognized what was happening. He had just thought of having a drink. This was the key moment in his addiction process. And yes, now that he thought about it, he was feeling very much trapped. His tendency in these situations was always to avoid conflict and that was just what he was feeling he had to do now, even though he really wanted to stay. No wonder he had thought of drinking! It fit the way he had come to understand his addiction: he was feeling helpless (and he realized at the same moment that he, himself, was creating this trap, by avoiding conflict with his friends). Following his usual pattern, he was about to reverse his sense of helplessness via a displaced behavior: drinking. He saw the parallels between this and the drinking he did after returning from the firm's meeting.

Although it takes longer to describe it, all of that passed through Eric's mind in a couple of seconds. But what could he do?

Greg said, "Hey Eric, you still in there?"

Eric glanced up at Greg, who was now standing up. "Hold on a sec," he said out loud.

"Okay," Eric thought to himself, "what if I don't drink. I'll have to do something else." He took a breath and it calmed him. "Okay," he thought again, "I guess the other choice is to not leave. Duh, that's pretty obvious. Well, I know myself well enough to know how hard it would be for me to go against the other guys. Maybe someday I'll work that out. I hope. But for now, I've got to find a way to deal with this or I'm going to drink. There's got to be a way to both not leave and not have a fight with the guys." He paused another moment, then nodded his head to himself.

"Listen," he said out loud to his friends, "you go on. I'm going to stay awhile."

"Really? You sure?" Andy said.

"Yes," Eric answered.

"Well, okay," Greg said, and turned to go.

"See ya later," Keith called as he walked up the aisle.

"Bye," Andy said. "If they come back and win, you can razz us later."

Eric waved and they left.

Eric did not drink that day. As usual, finding a practical way out of his trap was not the problem. Once he realized that his first fleeting thought of having a drink meant he was at the key moment in his addiction, he could see both how helpless he felt and what was making him feel so helpless. At that point the solution was obvious. It remained difficult, however, to enact the solution, because he felt so anxious about confronting his friends.

As he considered it, Eric realized he had limited himself to only two ways of dealing with the situation. He had thought, "I can either leave with the group as they want, or defy them by refusing to leave." Seeing it this way made this situation feel like the meeting at work—a risky confrontation with others who might turn on him.

And the fact was that Eric was not yet quite able to deal with such a clear confrontation. Perhaps, as he had thought to himself, he would be someday. But it turned out that it wasn't necessary to have this central issue all worked out in his mind yet.

He had found a way out of the helplessness trap by realizing that this didn't have to be one of his feared confrontations at all. Rather than either conceding to others or defying them, he could think of the situation as a peaceful decision: they could do what they wanted and he could do what he wanted. Instead of saying,

"No, I won't go," he could simply say, "You go on. I'm going to stay awhile."

Eric's solution was fine. But it is worth pausing for a moment to note that he didn't actually confront all the feelings this incident brought up for him.

What if he had been more comfortable being in conflict with his friends? Then he might have said, "You know I love baseball. I arranged to come today because I wanted to see the whole game. I definitely don't want to leave now. Stay at least until the ninth inning." That would have been an even more direct way for Eric to express himself. (And eventually, after he and I had worked together some more to understand his terror of conflict, Eric was able to do just that.)

But the main point for us here is that—even without resolving the underlying issues—simply being aware he was at the key moment in his addiction enabled him to come up with a good-enough solution. It was a solution that addressed his problem and resolved his sense of helplessness enough to prevent him from performing his addictive act.

KIMBERLY

Kimberly Powell could not stop eating. She had been eating compulsively for the past ten of her forty-five years, ever since she stopped drinking. She had once explained to a concerned friend that she couldn't stop eating for a very good reason. When she was a teenager she had used just about every street drug that existed, plus alcohol. Later, in her mid-twenties, she had stopped taking pills and just drank heavily. By the time she was in her mid-thirties and under multiple pressures to stop drinking, she had turned to food. When she stopped drinking her family and friends congratulated her and believed she had resolved her problems. Over the ensuing months and years, as her size went up and up, it became clear that they were wrong. Kimberly had stopped using alcohol and other drugs but, as she explained to her friend, this only meant she had a very good reason to eat: it was the only thing she had left.

Kimberly needed to have some addiction, no matter what form it took. She had grown up the third of five children. The first three, Kimberly and her older siblings, were all born within five years. Of these, the oldest and the next oldest—a girl and a boy— were, in Kimberly's judgment, the favorites of both parents. After Kimberly, there was a gap of five years before her little sister came along, followed by her baby brother when she was seven. From Kimberly's point of view, the "babies" formed the second favorite group. They were doted on by both parents, and Kimberly's older sister, and even her older brother until he became immersed in pre-teen things and found small children uninteresting.

Kimberly believed that every child had a special place in the family, except her. Her older sister was oldest, her older brother was the first boy, and then there were the upsettingly cute babies. Kimberly had been the baby herself for five years, but somehow that hadn't seemed to matter. Maybe it was because the first three had come so fast that being a baby had lost its novelty by the time she arrived. Maybe her parents were more rested by the time the new babies came. Whatever it was, Kimberly had felt she was the odd one out, forever. Whenever that old feeling emerged in her life she was at risk of acting on her addiction. To put it more accurately, whenever that feeling emerged she *had* to do something, and she had found a series of displacements—a series of "some-things"—over the years that produced her history of addictions.

Kimberly was an amateur potter. She had learned how to work with clay a few months earlier at an adult education class and found she loved the creativity of it and the pride of accomplishment when a bowl or a vase was finally finished and she could hold it in her hand and put it on a shelf. She didn't own any of her own equipment so she had to sign up to use one of the many potters' wheels and the kiln at the local high school where she had taken the pottery class. Since she was there pretty often, she was interested in the notices posted on the bulletin board about monthly meetings of local potters. She never attended because she had seen some of their work and it was far beyond anything she could produce.

However, after making what she felt was a particularly good bowl with a nice, even curve to it, she was emboldened to go to the pottery group. It was next Thursday evening, and she put it on her calendar.

The pottery room seemed particularly bright since the sky outside had darkened quickly this late in November. Kimberly didn't know any of the dozen or so people there, but to her relief the meeting routinely began with a series of introductions for the benefit of any new members, though it turned out she was the only newcomer. The discussion was led by a man about her age who introduced himself as a ceramics teacher in the Art Department of a local college. Once introductions were complete, conversation quickly turned to a technical question: the advantages of applying slip to bisqueware compared with applying it to greenware. Kimberly was lost immediately. For her, pottery was putting clay on a wheel, trying to make an object roughly resembling a bowl, firing it, glazing it, and praying. Still, she sat and listened, hoping the conversation would move on to something more relevant to her—like how to prevent bowls spinning crazily out of control on the wheel, and whether one could reuse the clay after it had splattered all over the wheel, the wall, and oneself. The conversation did eventually shift, but to another topic that she found just as abstruse.

After another ten minutes, the group leader sat down at one of the potters' wheels, gave a brief demonstration, and then asked everyone to get some clay from the community supply, select one of the room's wheels for themselves, and try to copy what he was doing. Kimberly hadn't expected this would be like a class but she was glad to move on to working with her hands. She began to try what the instructor had done while he started to walk around the group, talking to each of the people in the room. When he came to her, she had many questions. He was patient, but after what seemed a short time he said he had to talk with some of the others and moved off.

Kimberly's creation looked rough and amateurish compared with the work of the others who were also, after all, amateurs. She motioned to the instructor to come over again. He did, and she peppered him with more questions. Again, he was thoughtful and patient but again he left quickly. The third time Kimberly raised her hand to catch his attention, he was with another member of the group and he held up one finger: "Wait." It was awhile before he came over, and by then time was almost up for the evening. When he did walk over, it was just to mention a couple of things he saw she needed to work on, which Kimberly was aware were much more basic than the technical points he was showing the rest of the group.

When she returned home she began to eat.

The next day Kimberly felt awful, as usual. She knew she'd eaten a lot because the meeting had upset her. She had felt insignificant and second-rate at the meeting. She was the odd one out, again. But even being aware of her distress at the meeting had not been enough to stop her bingeing later.

Like Eric in the previous example, after this episode Kimberly had the chance to learn about the steps we've discussed. Unlike Eric, however, she decided not to wait until a circumstance arose to test her new understanding of her addiction; she went out and created it on purpose.

It was a couple of months later and Kimberly was making a point of looking at the notices on the bulletin board at the high school to find the next meeting of the pottery group. She was still interested in joining. But this time she would be prepared.

It wasn't that her pottery skills had improved very much. The tops of her vases were still as likely to collapse as stay up. She still came in to the high school to see her work after it had been fired in the kiln only to find a jumble of pieces on top of a piece of paper with her name and the note: "Sorry, this cracked and fell apart during firing. Come see one of us to find out what you did wrong." No, it wasn't her improved skills that made her more prepared. It was that she had figured out just how her feelings had led to her eating after the first meeting.

When she looked back at that meeting, Kimberly recognized that she had started to think about eating while she was still there, but she hadn't recognized this as the key moment. Consequently, even though she was aware she was upset, she didn't stop to consider whether there was some direct action she could take at that point to deal with her feelings.

Later, when she thought about the meeting, she could see that it wasn't just that she was technically out of her league. The real problem was that as soon as the meeting began and the conversation was over her head, she had experienced her form of overwhelming helplessness—that old sense of being less than others and unimportant. Immediately, she had been filled with desperation to be seen and heard. Then when the group moved on to working with clay, she found herself grasping for the instructor's time and attention beyond what was realistic to expect in a group; she could see that now. The instructor had kept leaving her before all her questions were answered because she was asking so much, not because he considered her less important. Without meaning to, Kimberly had set up just the situation she feared. It was all the worse for her because her questions were not only to be reassured that the instructor considered her just as important as the others, they were also an attempt to learn a lot, quickly, so she could rise to their level. It was another way to help her feel that she belonged, which had backfired terribly.

Kimberly arrived a few minutes early for the next pottery meeting. She wanted to have a chance to talk with some of the other members before the session began. It was one way to deal with her feelings of being left out. As the group gathered for discussion, Kimberly awaited her turn to introduce herself. When it came to her, she gave a little speech that she had prepared: "Hello, I'm Kimberly. I was here a couple of months ago. I'm a new potter. I only started working with clay about six months ago. I'm hoping I can join this group regularly to learn more about making things, but also to get to know other people who are interested in pottery-making. I probably won't have too much to contribute to your discussions, but I hope it's okay that I come." The response was immediate. "Of course you can come! We all started the same way." "Welcome! Believe me, you're not going to be so far behind. I have a million questions about *my* work." "We're glad you're here." Later, the group split up to practice a technique and Kimberly again found herself struggling. This time, when the instructor came over she looked at her attempt and said, "Well, this is a mess. I wonder if I could do a simpler version of it." He smiled and suggested she work on a small part of the whole technique.

After the meeting, as she was giving her good-byes, Kimberly was glad to say that she'd see them all next month.

There was nothing special about the way Kimberly handled this second meeting. She acted in the friendly, open way she usually did—the way she behaved when she didn't feel overwhelmed by the major emotional concerns of her life. As with the other people we've seen, once she had learned how her addiction worked it was easy for her to find solutions to what had seemed an impossible trap—one that would have led inexorably to her addictive act. Of course, it would have been even better for her if she weren't troubled by her lifelong feelings of unimportance and worthlessness, and Kimberly did pursue psychotherapy to ultimately resolve those issues. But like Eric in the previous example, even before accomplishing that, she was able to gain control over her addiction.

HOW TO FIND SHORT-TERM SOLUTIONS

Hearing these stories you might wonder if taking a more direct action when you feel helpless is really so easy to do. It's true that these solutions are pretty obvious once you see the problem. But can you get yourself to do them?

Whether you can break through your addiction depends on whether you can find a "good-enough" solution to your helplessness trap. That was what Eric did when he spoke up about wanting to stay at the ball game. He still couldn't be completely forthright with his friends about how he felt, but the action he took was *good enough* to relieve his sense of powerlessness and keep him from drinking. Here are some general strategies for good-enough solutions:

- **Just go away.** One option available in many situations is to simply leave—to walk away. Naturally this won't always work, since leaving a predicament could very well increase feelings of helplessness. But sometimes it's a perfectly good and simple way to manage your helplessness trap. In Kimberly's story, during the first pottery club meeting when she felt so trapped, she could have just walked out. That wouldn't have been as direct or helpful as what she did during the second meeting when she came right out and said how she felt, but by leaving she would have been giving herself a freedom that could have prevented her eating episode. Being free is an antidote to feeling helpless.

- **Do what you like.** Leaving a situation can also mean freeing yourself to have something you like; doing what you really want to do is a good way to reverse feelings of being forced into doing something you don't want to do. If you recall Marjorie and her party, she was always serving others in her life. Since she did that so much, she often took her drugs. In the long run, the best thing for her, of course, would have been to work out her excessive need to serve people. But in the meantime, her chronic feelings of disempowerment would have been helped just by making sure she did more for herself. Marjorie loved to take photographs, but she rarely took them because she made her life too busy taking care of others. Not getting to enjoy her hobby was a source of persistent aggravation, even sadness, for her. And it contributed to her persistent need to take pills. If she had understood how her emotional life worked and how important it was for her to give herself the chance to do the things she loved, she could have been sure to carve out time for her photography.

That wouldn't have solved everything, but it would have been a simple way to decrease the strain in her life that kept leading to her addiction. It also would not have called upon Marjorie to do what she was unable to do just yet—to pay attention to how she felt during the times she was overwhelmed by her need to serve others. Even before she fully learned the mechanism of her addiction—the issues behind it, and how and why the urge arose—she could reduce her chances of taking drugs by creating opportunities to do what she liked at less emotionally stressful times.

- **It's never too late.** Another way to act more directly when you're not prepared to fully address your helplessness is to act after the fact. There is often an opportunity later to say or do something you wish you had said or done at the time. After Kimberly left the first meeting and felt so upset, if she had paused to notice that she was headed for her addiction, she might have instead written a letter or an e-mail to the director of the pottery club explaining what she ended up saying at the second meeting. Doing this would have been late, but not necessarily too late, any more than it was too late for her to return to the meeting the second time. There is nothing wrong with examining and addressing your feelings of helplessness after the fact; nobody is watching your life with a stopwatch. In Eric's story, after he sat silently through his firm's meeting because he was afraid to speak up, he too could have written down his views on the issues discussed and either sent them to the appropriate firm officers or even just prepared them as a memo to debate in a day or so. Understandably, it can be hard to do these after-the-fact actions because you are that much further down the path toward your addiction, and likely experiencing more and more compulsion toward it. But the possibility of acting after the fact is worth keeping in mind as a fallback.

As you practice using these tools you may want to try them in the safest possible situations first, and give yourself some leeway in how direct your actions are. Remember, you don't have to come up with the best possible solution, just one that does the job.

HOW TO FIND SHORT-TERM SOLUTIONS
IN MORE COMPLEX SITUATIONS

What can make it more difficult to take a direct action under certain circumstances is either that your behavior is realistically restricted by outside factors, or your fear of the consequences is too great to take even partial actions to fight your feelings of helplessness. When this happens, you need a bit more imagination and tolerance of sad or anxious feelings to find alternatives in the key moment, since the immediate and simplest solutions may not be available. Here is an example:

GIL

Gil was a heroin addict. He was on the brink of losing his relationship with his girlfriend, in part because—after he had nearly died twice—she could no longer live with the fear of him overdosing. She was very important to him, so he was facing an awful loss—the sort of traumatic loss that earlier in his life had led to his addiction in the first place. When his girlfriend began to strongly hint that she was going to break up with him, his urge to use heroin was nearly overwhelming.

But what sorts of short-term solutions were available to Gil? What could he do to address his larger sense of helplessness at the looming loss of his girlfriend, so that he would not have to reach for that old "solution" to his problems? He knew that talking with his girlfriend wouldn't change her mind at this point. Promising to stop using, no matter how sincere he was, would also not matter now. He couldn't magically substitute another person for her. Was there nothing that could keep him from his addiction?

There is always some way to stop moving down the addictive

path. But in hard cases like these, finding it requires stepping back and taking whatever time you can to think about it.

Gil was facing a loss that would be difficult for anyone. He would have to experience a period of grief, since grief is a normal reaction to loss. This was harder for him than others because of his personal history of multiple early losses. Because of these losses, over the course of his life he had dealt with grief by trying any way he could to avoid it. In fact, it was just this lifelong struggle to manage the pain of grief that led him to develop a heroin addiction. Now the only way he would be able to keep from using heroin was to focus on handling his grief.

This may seem like an obvious point, but it's not. Gil was not focusing on how to deal with his grief; he was focusing on the problem of losing his girlfriend. And these are two different things.

Focus on Your Feelings, Not the External Reality

For Gil, losing his girlfriend was an aspect of *external reality* over which he had no control at this point. He actually was helpless about that. But there were things he could do about his *grief*, since grief was a feeling inside of him. Nobody could replace his girlfriend, but he did have other people he could talk with to help him bear his feelings. Some people facing serious losses find great comfort in speaking with a religious leader, or a valued older person who has more experience with life. Others rely mainly on family or friends—to speak with or to live with during a hard time. Just planning to do one of these things could help Gil, since making a plan, in itself, is a way to feel empowered rather than helpless.

If he focused on dealing with his grief rather than on the loss of his girlfriend, Gil might also have been able to develop a better perspective on his loss. He was losing someone he cared about, but he still had others he cared about and who cared about him. As we all know, when enough time passes after a loss, we find that we go on; life continues and can still have its joys. Mourning is not the same as being trapped in a cave, even though it can feel that way. It is awful but not permanent. If Gil had thought about managing his grief as his central problem, rather than about losing his girlfriend, he might have been able to step far enough away from the experience of utter helplessness that always led to his addiction.

The end of a relationship or the loss of a loved one is not the only sort of loss beyond one's control. The events that set off the addictive process might be the loss of a job or even a career. It could be a move from the place you love, the loss of an opportunity, or a serious injury. It could be any disappointment that is deeply meaningful to you. These would all be situations in which there is no practical way to reverse the problem; you are truly helpless over the reality. In all these cases the approach would be the same: take time to sit back and focus on your feelings rather than just the external facts.

Focusing on your feelings is actually just one form of observing yourself, and when you do this (imagine floating ten feet above your body and looking down) you may feel you are no longer *in* the trap. This gives you a bit of time to work out a more direct way to deal with your situation while empowering you in the process.

Here is a somewhat different example:

MARY

Mary had been dating her boyfriend, Chad, for two years. Although they fought from time to time, at twenty-eight years old, this was the longest she had ever dated someone. This relationship seemed like it was a keeper. Until, that is, her birthday arrived and it turned out Chad had forgotten about it. She had been talking about her birthday for the past month. She had even hinted at what might be a nice present from the man with whom she had been so close for two years. How could he forget?

Mary suffered with alcoholism, and responded to the situation by drinking for two days straight, and missing work. Once she stopped drinking, she called Chad and told him they were through.

Mary was deeply hurt. From her standpoint, Chad had proved that he was not the man for her. Forgetting her birthday was a wake-up call. He was showing how self-centered he was. He could never be a caring, reliable partner.

Mary's hurt was made worse by the fact that Chad was not the first boyfriend who had ended up being someone different from who she had thought, and hoped, he was. Now more than ever, Mary wondered if she could ever find a man who would really love her. It was something she had been depressed about for a long time, a trap from which there seemed no escape.

Now and in the past, her drinking was precipitated by feelings like these; it was a displaced response, meant to reverse the overwhelming helplessness she so often felt. In addition to drinking, she also reacted directly (out of her sense of helplessness and rage) by telling Chad she didn't want to see him again.

As in Gil's case, Mary was dealing with a real event—Chad forgetting her birthday—that could not be undone by any direct action on her part. At this key moment, she was deeply upset, but the question she could have asked herself was: What makes this so upsetting for me? She had a history of disappointing relationships; that made this relationship extra important. This man, she had hoped, would be the keeper. Beyond this reality, though, she saw Chad's forgetfulness as an indication that she would never find anyone who could love her. It was this personal interpretation of Chad's blunder that triggered her addiction, not Chad's blunder itself. If Mary paused and refocused away from Chad and his failures, she could recognize what his forgetting *meant* to her.

Without letting Chad off the hook, she could have considered her sensitivity to emotional injuries like this one. Looking at their relationship this way, perhaps she would recall the times Chad did remember what was important to her. Maybe there were times he had been spontaneously giving and caring beyond what she expected. That would give her some perspective on her feelings now. Or, she might decide that Chad was really the insensitive guy she feared. In this case she would have accurately placed the problem mostly in Chad, not herself. Ending the relationship with him might be the most sensible reaction.

Either way, Mary could see that she had jumped from the experience with Chad to the generalization that nobody would ever love her—her old issue. Noticing that she had made this mental jump would have alerted her to step back and think about where these overwhelming feelings were coming from. With this perspective she could break from her helplessness trap, making it unlikely that she would turn to drinking.

The Importance of Anticipation

The cases above, involving irretrievable losses, are especially tough because there are no clear, practical actions that can repair or undo the losses. There was nothing Gil could do, for example, that would bring his girlfriend back. It is especially important in these situations, therefore, to recognize in advance when they might arise. Once you have become aware of the defenses you use, and the sorts of issues that produce helplessness traps for you, you can think about situations and events that may precipitate these traps, and what your response to them would be. Anticipating these events is easier when you consider that there are often hints well in advance that they are coming.

Gil and his girlfriend, for example, had been fighting a long time—about his heroin use and other problems. He could not have been wholly blindsided by a breakup. If he had recognized his deep-seated sensitivity to being left—that this kind of loss was overwhelming for him, and was linked to his addiction—he could have anticipated his intense urge to use heroin. The anticipation itself would have provided some protection against his compulsion to use the drug.

Mary likewise could have recognized that feelings of being unloved and unlovable were overwhelming for her. With this in mind—and knowing that she suffered with alcoholism—she could have thought ahead to the possibility of a breakup with Chad, and the risk this posed for her drinking. If she had sat down and imagined how a breakup would feel, identifying it as the kind of event that usually precipitated her addiction, she would have been far less likely to drink.

Because it is so valuable to recognize the key moment— the earliest point at which you begin to think about performing your addictive act—you can help yourself by imagining this moment yourself. You can do this by anticipating the circumstances in which it would occur.

All the people we've seen in this chapter had certain emotional sensitivities that became overwhelming under relevant circumstances. Recognizing how these sensitivities led to their addictions allowed them to figure out short-term practical solutions, or to develop a perspective on why their feelings were so strong at those moments. These short-term strategies—such as removing yourself from situations you know are likely to engender helplessness, doing things for yourself if you have to deprive yourself elsewhere, acting "after the fact" to reverse feelings of helplessness, focusing on the feelings aroused by events rather than the events themselves, and anticipating and imagining potential situations that will feel overwhelming—will help free you from your helplessness traps.

Now we can take one final step. If you know and understand the *roots* of your helplessness trap, you can eliminate feelings of helplessness and powerlessness where they begin. Without an overwhelming sense of helplessness when you face triggering situations, you can break your addiction forever. Let's see how to do this in Step 7.

How to Deal with Addiction in the Long Term

We know that emotional experiences can give rise to feelings of intolerable helplessness, and that addiction works as a symptom to reverse this helplessness. We have discussed short-term strategies to find more direct ways to handle feelings of helplessness when they occur. Now it is time to consider a more basic question. Is it possible to reduce or eliminate the feelings of intolerable helplessness behind addictive behavior so that they don't overwhelm you? We saw in Step 6 that helpless feelings at the key moment in addiction can be reduced by anticipating when these moments will occur. Since there are usually hints of trouble before the final overwhelming event (the breakup of a relationship, a job loss, etc.), these hints can help you to anticipate what is coming. Now we'll see how knowing the roots of your helplessness allows you to predict when you will be at high risk for your addiction very, very far in advance—even before there are any hints. If you can understand yourself this well then you have the opportunity to end your addiction forever.

As you gather experience with the techniques we've discussed—

paying close attention to what is happening at the key moments when you first consider your addictive act—you will notice a common theme behind these moments. You will see that, repeatedly, you are terrified to be left out, or you feel humiliated or disparaged by others, or you feel you're being treated as if you are weak, or you're infuriated because you feel you aren't being heard—or it might be you're made anxious by success, or certain situations remind you of past traumas, or something else that is individual to you. Whatever it is, you can know it. It will be the central problematic theme of your life—an emotional vulnerability specific to you that surfaces again and again, and results in feelings of helplessness and powerlessness (what we have called the "helplessness trap"). Once you become familiar with this theme you will be able to think through these perilous occasions very far in advance—much farther in advance than the kinds of anticipation that we saw in Step 6. You will be able to avoid going through the stage of having addictive urges at all.

Let's revisit Mary from the last chapter to illustrate this point. You may recall that Mary felt she could never find somebody who would love her. Mary had held this conviction for a long time—since her childhood (and of course long before she ever met her boyfriend Chad or before Chad could make the mistake of forgetting her birthday). But Mary had not recognized the deep-rootedness of this feeling. She had not identified it as the core emotional vulnerability in her life. If she had, what a difference that would have made! When Chad forgot her birthday, she would not have had such a devastating reaction, because she would have seen that her response was, at least in part, due to her own belief that she was unlovable. Aware of this long and deeply held belief, she could even have *predicted*, much earlier, that *eventually* she would experience some disappointment in this relationship. And she would know that when that time came, she would experience it as another proof of how unlovable she was; consequently, she would feel helplessly trapped. Being aware of this, she would have been able to predict her urge to turn to a drink far in advance.

By knowing herself this well, Mary would also have seen the lesser events along the pathway to the final breakup as the warnings that they were. Her fights with Chad over the years before their ultimate falling-out would have brought her old underlying vulnerability to mind. She would have seen that it was not only the outward details of each fight that so upset her, but also her lifelong feeling of inadequacy—of being unlovable—that was being stirred up. And, knowing she suffered with an addiction, she would realize that it was especially important for her to pay attention to signals that her old vulnerability was being aroused.

If you suffer with an addiction, then, like Mary, you have a special incentive to become an expert on the subject of yourself, particularly the roots of your feelings of helplessness. Like Mary, your ability to be free of your addiction forever depends on it.

Here is another example:

DONALD

Donald knew he was a failure. As a child he had been a mediocre student in school. It wasn't because he couldn't keep up; it was because he didn't pay much attention and didn't work hard. His parents and teachers viewed him as lazy, and told him so. Donald agreed. He scraped through high school and did enroll in college, but once there his use of crack cocaine increased dramatically, and he dropped out. After college he continued smoking cocaine regularly and lost several jobs through inattentiveness or because he simply didn't show up the day after he had been awake all night getting high. To his surprise, despite this history several women had showed persistent interest in him. Each, however, finally gave up on him when he seemed more concerned with smoking crack than being with them.

Donald had never really tried to stop using cocaine, any more than he had ever really tried to study at school or work at his jobs. He hardly stopped to think about his life at all. He was what he was. If he ever had any question about being a failure (and he couldn't remember any time he doubted this view), his lifelong experiences kept proving to him that he was correct. His failure was as much a part of him as his arms or legs.

But even with his sense of the grim constancy of his life and future, Donald could not help noticing that there was one thing that was not staying the same in his life. Time was moving on. Throughout his youth and all those years of school, and even into his twenties, time hadn't seemed to matter.

However, now he was twenty-nine and his next birthday was coming up. There was something about leaving his twenties that got his attention. If there were any chance at all of changing the rest of his life, it ought to happen before he became old, he thought. And, in his mind, thirty was definitely getting old. So Donald finally began to give some thought to his cocaine use.

At the time, he was looking for another new job, since he had recently been fired from his last one. He had been working in sales, so he figured he'd start there. He began the job search process he knew so well—looking up Internet listings, e-mailing his résumé, getting back in touch with the headhunter firms he had used before, calling a few people who might network him into at least a first meeting.

Two weeks later he got his first hit—an invitation for a telephone interview, which he knew was basically a screen to decide whether to schedule a later face-to-face meeting. Donald was bright and verbal and came across well on the phone. Indeed, he had always done well in interviews, which helped explain why he kept finding jobs despite his troubled work history. On the phone this time he was impressive again, and a face-to-face interview was set up for the following week.

The next Tuesday when he arrived at the company, Donald was asked to meet with three different management people. One would be his immediate supervisor if he were hired and two others were executives who seemed to be higher up in the company, judging from their titles.

He was there for two hours. One higher-up quizzed him unusually carefully about his previous work experiences and why he had left them, and his persistence surprised Donald and left him feeling somewhat unprepared. On the whole, though, Donald thought the meetings went well and he was confident when he returned home that evening. Getting jobs had never been the problem.

Several days went by without Donald hearing from this company. He knew they were almost certainly interviewing other applicants, particularly in what was a difficult job market, but he was still disappointed. When he left the interviews, he thought he would hear good news the very next day, as had happened to him once or twice before.

When a week passed, Donald began to worry. He decided to call the company to find out what was happening. He reached the man he had originally spoken with on the phone, someone in Human Resources.

Donald gave his name and asked the status of his application. The man didn't seem to register his name at first, but then he said, "Oh, yes. I'm sorry we didn't get back to you. We've filled that position. There were just so many applicants that we couldn't call them all to tell them. I'm sorry."

Donald hung up. He had been turned down for jobs before, but somehow this time it was harder to take. He had been giving more and more thought to making changes in his life. Getting this job was supposed to have been the first step toward a fresh start.

As soon as he put down the telephone he thought of using

some of the cocaine he still had in his apartment. He knew it was what he always did on these occasions.

Exactly what he meant by "these occasions" wasn't clear to him, however. All he knew was that this moment felt like a lot of the other times when he used drugs.

Would he use again now? What about his fresh start? Donald mulled it over.

It was at this point that Donald became stuck in a way we're familiar with; he began to think about not getting this job, and how that set him back. By focusing on losing the job opportunity, he was ignoring what it *meant* to him to lose it—the feelings this loss aroused in him. Consequently, he couldn't find ways to deal with his disappointment, anger, and helplessness—emotions he could address by taking actions of some kind, even though there was nothing he could do about losing the job itself. In focusing on the event instead of his *experience* of it, he couldn't find ways to gain perspective on his feelings or ways to deal with them.

What happened next wasn't surprising, then. Even though he was trying his hardest to stop using cocaine, and even though he did struggle with using when the urge first arose, his sense of helplessness overruled every other thought. He grabbed the bag of coke from his stash in the back of his bedroom dresser drawer and set about smoking it.

Donald's focus on the event rather than his feelings was actually the last problem in what had been an invisible march toward his addiction. Because he had not considered the feelings that plagued him throughout his life or understood their connection to his addiction, he couldn't foresee that he would be at high risk of performing his addictive behavior if the job didn't come through. If he could have anticipated, from self-knowledge, that not getting the job would be a key moment on the path to his addiction, he could have prevented this addictive episode.

FOUR WAYS THAT BEING AN EXPERT ON YOURSELF ENABLES YOU TO DEAL WITH ADDICTION FOREVER

1. Predicting recurrence. As we have seen, identifying the common emotional theme behind your overwhelming feelings of helplessness is essential to predict its recurrence. Once you identify this theme, you are able to anticipate "high risk" situations that make you feel trapped and lead to addictive urges.

In Donald's case, events that reasserted his image of himself as a failure precipitated overwhelming feelings of helplessness. These moments exposed a deep emotional vulnerability in his life. But Donald had not recognized the common emotional theme connecting these moments. If he had, it would have been clear to him in advance that a rejection in his job search would be unbearable for him—proof once again, in his eyes, that he was a failure. Beyond this, he would have known even *before* he began his job search, perhaps months before, that he would be at risk of smoking cocaine. Knowing this risk so far in advance, he would have been emotionally prepared for it. *He would have had a good chance of never even reaching the stage of having addictive urges.*

The story of Marjorie and her weekend party offers another example of how you can use deeper self-knowledge to predict addictive episodes very far in advance. You may recall that we traced the key moment—when she first thought about using her pills—to five days before she actually took them. But now we can add something to this story. If Marjorie had been aware of her history of trapping herself by overdoing for others, she could have recognized the risk of returning to her pill use months earlier, when she first had the *idea* of throwing a party! As a result, she could have made decisions right then that would have averted the key moment altogether.

2. Stepping out of the trap in key moments. By identifying the common emotional theme behind your feelings of helplessness, you can see how this theme makes you prone to experience events as repetitions of old painful problems, whether the situation realistically warrants it or not.

In Donald's case, because of his terrible disparagement of himself he tended to experience losses and disappointments as if they were new proofs of his being a failure. Experiencing disappointments this way led him to have an extreme emotional reaction when they occurred. If he had been aware of this pattern, then the despair and anger provoked by his rejected job application would have alerted him that his old issues were afoot. The arousal of these extreme feelings alone would have given him cause to stop and think. With this awareness he would have been able to separate his current disappointment from his overwhelming, lifelong sense of failure. His current disappointment would then become more manageable.

Mary's case offers another example: the intensity of her reaction when Chad forgot her birthday could have cued Mary to the fact that her lifelong feelings of being unlovable were being set off. This would put Chad's forgetting into perspective, and keep Mary from falling into her helplessness trap.

3. Understanding your life. By understanding the emotions underlying your feelings of helplessness, you gain a greater perspective on your behavior not only in the present, but also in the past.

Donald not only felt like a failure, but he had lived out the reality of being a failure by paying practically no attention to the way he was leading his life for his first twenty-nine years. His conscious view was that it made no difference for him to lose job after job since he was doomed never to succeed anyway. More deeply, and without being aware of it, he was making these destructive decisions out of an unconscious rage about never being given credit for what he did. He wasn't just a failure; he was aggressively a failure. Every time he failed he was in effect saying to his bosses and any other authorities, "You're never going to think I'm doing a good job anyway, so why should I bother? You treat me like I'm worthless. Well, I'll treat you the same way. You can pay me but you're going to get very little work from me." Sadly, by making himself fail repeatedly he created and re-created precisely the old helpless trap of his childhood. Then, because it was repeated over the years, his identity as a failure felt more and more real to him. The longer the pattern persisted, the more Donald experienced it as just the way his life was, rather than something he constantly had a hand in reinforcing. His addiction was a part of this cycle, since he reversed his feeling of helplessness via the displaced act of taking drugs. The more he reinforced his own identity as a failure, the more he used drugs to manage his feelings of helplessness, and the more his drug use itself contributed to his failing. If Donald had been aware of the central issue of his life and how it had affected the way he lived from day to day, he could have started to make sense of how he arrived at his current state, and how to get out of it.

4. Turning the tables on your addiction: using it to become an expert on yourself. If you don't know the central problematic issues in your life already, listening to your feelings and thoughts at the key moment of despair and rage will help you to discover them.

Paying close attention to your feelings every time you are in your helplessness trap has another advantage: *It is the easiest way to know what personal vulnerability precipitates your addiction.*

If Donald had listened to his thoughts and feelings in the painful moment his job application was rejected, he would have had the chance to discover his profound, deep-rooted sense of failure. He would surely have recognized the long history of these thoughts and feelings through his entire life. It would be a short step from this realization to an understanding that his reaction now, his sense of being a failure, was his core vulnerability. He was not feeling trapped and enraged just because he didn't get the job. It was because this event was reviving an old theme in his life.

A FINAL NOTE

As I've suggested through many case stories, problems intense enough to lead to addiction generally have a long history in people's lives. What makes the particular vulnerabilities that lead to *your* addiction so powerful for you?

To find why the common theme behind your addiction carries the emotional intensity it does, you will need to cast back over your life and the important relationships that make you who you are. You are looking for clues that will help answer the question, "What in my life makes me sensitive to" being left out, or feeling put down, and so on. You may have already been thinking about this as you have read about the backgrounds of the people I've described. Of course, if you already know the central concerns and issues in your life, then you can more easily think back to their origins. If you are unclear about your main emotional issues, then you can begin by looking for areas of sadness or anxiety in your past. And as we've seen just above, you can focus on the feelings that arise when you have addictive urges to figure out what emotional challenge or experience is at the heart of your addiction. This may feel like work, and it is. As I've said all along, it is not necessary to fully work out these emotional issues in order to conquer your addictive behavior. But the more you know about yourself, about what makes you tick, the better prepared you will be to predict and manage your addiction.

And, of course, knowing yourself better can help not only with your addiction but also with the quality of your life. Addiction is, after all, only a symptom of things that bother you. And like other ways of managing emotional concerns, it can be understood and mastered.

The next chapter gives you the chance to put your knowledge of these steps to work with some new case examples.

Test Yourself

Now that you've read about the seven steps to take control of your addiction, here is a chance to put this knowledge into practice. I've been describing the stories of people with addictions and discussing what each story tells us about the addictive process. In this chapter, I will tell you the stories of several more people but without any commentary. For each case I would like you to think about the following four questions:

1. What are the underlying emotional themes that lead to the experience of helplessness and, in turn, its addictive solution?
2. What defenses does this person use to keep him or her from seeing the key moment?
3. What is the key moment on this person's path to addiction?
4. What more direct alternative actions could he or she have taken in place of the addictive act?

You may find it helpful to jot down your answers. I will discuss the answers to these questions at the end of each case.

Luke

Dr. Luke Greene walked into his office in the Radiology Department of his hospital. *Trudged* in was more like it. His shoulders were slumped, as usual. He carried his briefcase as though it were the weight of the world.

He sunk into his chair. Luke was aware that his colleagues sometimes joked about his depressed outlook, saying that radiology was perfect for him since he seemed to live in a life of shadows. But it wasn't funny to him. Life really was depressing, and always had been.

When he started drinking more heavily, as a radiology resident just a year out of medical school, it was for the express purpose of lifting his mood. This appeared to work well, so he continued, and increased his drinking until it was a ritual at the end of every day, the only exception being when he would be on call again within eight hours. When his training was over, his on-call time sharply decreased and his drinking increased. Now, at forty years old, he was drinking enough every night to have a mild tremor each morning when he awoke. He knew that was an early symptom of withdrawal from alcohol and he treated it with a shot of whiskey at breakfast. He believed this was not enough to impair him, especially since he could sit at his desk answering e-mail for the first hour of the day, and it would get him to work without shaking.

Luke worked hard. He always had, and his current position as assistant chief of his hospital department spoke to that. He did good work and was well-respected. His private life was less successful, however. Unmarried, he had been in three major relationships over the years. Drinking was a factor in spoiling each of them, but it wasn't the only cause. At the start of each relationship Luke's intelligence and kindness had trumped his persistent gloominess. The women who cared about him either believed his downcast mood would fade on its own or they could make it go away. One woman had tearfully told Luke directly, just before leaving him, that she had thought her love for him would be enough to make him happy.

And he had tried to be happy with these women. The truth was that he had loved each of them and the end of each relationship had been deeply painful. But his depressed worldview was not in his control.

Luke did not like to turn to others for help. But working in a hospital made it a little easier for him to ask a friend who worked there, a psychiatrist, if he thought an antidepressant might help him. His colleague agreed to prescribe one, and for six months Luke had taken the medication. Unfortunately, it had not changed his usual feelings. The psychiatrist friend, who had known Luke as a colleague for years and was well aware of how burdened he always looked, told Luke that he was not surprised. He said that the fact that Luke had been depressed for as long as he had known him indicated that his mood had more to do with the way he viewed life and himself, rather than a temporary shift in his brain chemistry—the kind of depression that usually responds beautifully to these medicines. He suggested that Luke talk to another member of the Psychiatry Department about getting some therapy, but Luke didn't do this. His normal pessimism led him to think that would probably not do any good, either. He left this experience with the impression that even professional help couldn't improve his life.

Yet, perhaps paradoxically, he had never been the kind of person who gave up. Throughout his depressing life he had trudged on and worked to get to his next goal. Although he was barely conscious of it, behind this hard work was a flickering hope that getting to that next step might finally make him happy, even though it had never worked out that way. So, now that he believed psychological help had nothing to offer him, he told himself that he had to work his hardest on his own to stop drinking.

Luke still held on to the idea that his drinking helped him to get through life, mostly because his life had so little else that gave him any relief. But after unsuccessfully trying to stop on several occasions he had reached a point where he could no longer deny that his drinking was more of a problem than a solution. This recognition, coupled now with his belief that there was nothing else he could do to address his depression, made ending drinking his number one priority. He felt confident that if he really set his mind to it he could stop drinking permanently. Hard work had always been his strength.

Luke had often acted as his own doctor, since he didn't like to ask his colleagues or others for help, and he knew that he could safely taper himself off alcohol over a few days. He made a schedule and he stuck with it. For the following couple of weeks he was alcohol-free.

He noticed right away that he felt better physically, and that did improve his mood a bit. But as the days went by this good feeling began to fade. By the second week of his abstinence, while he still felt better physically, it was clear to him that he was returning to his old self. He could feel the weight of the world on him, again.

Still, at least he didn't have both his emotional problems *and* his drinking, and he remained abstinent.

Almost a month after his last drink, Luke was sitting in his office at the hospital when the phone rang. It was his department chief, asking Luke to step over to his office for a minute. When he arrived, the chief motioned him to a chair.

CHIEF: Well, I have some good news and some bad news.
LUKE: Which one has to do with me?
CHIEF (*laughs*): The good news is for you. I've been offered a
   post as visiting professor at a terrific academic hospital on
   the Coast and I'm going to take it, for a year. So, I suppose

that is good news for me, but it also means I have to leave
this place for a while and I'm going to miss it.

LUKE: That's great. You've earned it.

CHIEF: Thanks. But the completely good news is that this
makes you acting chair for the year. I think you'll find
that with this on your resume you can move just about
anywhere if you ever want, plus it comes with a bump in
salary and in your academic title at the medical school—
and that's permanent even after I return.

LUKE: Well, that is very good. Thank you.

CHIEF: Not at all. There's nobody else who could do this job
here as well as you, and you deserve it.

When Luke left the chief's office he had a strange mix of feelings. This was certainly good news. But Luke felt the old depressive feelings worsening. Did he really deserve this? He had only
been assistant chief for a year and a half. The chief was about
twenty years older and nationally known. Why did they pick
him to fill in? Sure, he was assistant, but to fill the position for
a whole year, they could have recruited someone who was much
better known.

By the time Luke returned to his own office he began to think
about having a drink. This made no sense to him at all. He had
been abstinent now for nearly a month and he thought he was finally past drinking. Besides, why would he think about drinking
now? This promotion was very good news.

Luke buried himself in work the rest of the day and didn't
have to think more about this sudden change. On the way home
he passed the liquor store. When he had stopped drinking the
prior month he had also discarded all of the whiskey he still had
at home. Luke slowed the car, and then turned into the liquor
store's parking lot. He switched off the ignition and sat there.
"This is insane," he told himself. "I should be feeling great now.

Acting chief. That's pretty damn good." Then he got out of the car and went into the store. He brought home a bottle of his brand of whiskey and began drinking right after he came in the door.

Luke grew up in an apartment house in a large city. He was the third child in his family after his brother, Stan, who was six years older, and his sister, Sandra, who was four years older. Some time before Luke came into the world his father lost his longtime job at a shoe manufacturing plant. The family had struggled after that, moving twice when Luke's dad found work in other cities. They went into serious debt, and for a few months they relied on what was then the new food-stamp program to provide for their two small children, Stan and Sandra. Then, just before Luke was born, his father landed a good job in a growing company. Over the next couple of years, while still sacrificing anything that might be considered a luxury—including the toys Luke's older siblings craved—they crawled out of debt. By the time Luke was three-and-a-half years old, they were on their feet. Luke never remembered the hardships his family had suffered; he had been too young to sense the family's early struggles.

But his family remembered, and though his parents had no intention of hurting Luke, he often heard from them about what they had been through and how grateful he should be for having escaped it. His siblings were more direct. Both of them saw him as unfairly lucky. At Christmas he always had plenty of new toys, and even though by that time they too received nice things, they never let him forget that he was the "spoiled" one. Luke's parents might have done more to protect him from his older siblings, but in their minds this treatment was probably good for him. They, too, believed Luke might be spoiled by having been born after the worst times were over.

Luke got this message loud and clear. Over the years, his response was to work hard at school or at chores around the house, to show that he did appreciate how fortunate he was. He became a serious child, not smiling much. Outside the family, he earned admiration from his teachers and coaches for his dedication and perseverance. But, oddly to those around him, he never seemed to derive much pleasure from the awards he received for either schoolwork or athletic accomplishments. He seemed to have accepted the judgment of his parents and siblings that he had already been given too much. He was spoiled and didn't deserve more.

When he began drinking as a radiology resident, it was a welcome relief. He felt a burden was lifted. It was no wonder it took him so many years to decide that drinking was a bad idea for him; it had seemed like such a good thing.

The day after he finished off half the whiskey bottle he'd bought at the liquor store, Luke woke feeling terrible. He had a headache and felt slightly sick. But he was also filled with confusion and regret. He had thought his drinking problem was solved. Even though he hadn't been able to stop when he'd tried in the past, he believed he had never really put his mind to it as he did this time. And he had been perfectly able to not drink for weeks. Why would he drink now? Like much of the rest of his emotional life, this simply did not make sense.

ANSWERS TO DISCUSSION QUESTIONS

1. What are the underlying emotional themes that led to Luke's experience of helplessness and, in turn, its addictive solution?

Luke grew up with a sense that he did not deserve what was given to him. His parents told him regularly that he should be grateful for not having gone through the troubles of the family before he was born and during his first couple of years. His older siblings picked up his parents' message and reinforced it by taunting Luke for being the spoiled child. Sadly, though his parents had worked hard to provide a better life for Luke, their repeated message that he had a better deal than the rest of his family made his life much worse. He grew up with a burden of unworthiness and guilt from which there seemed no way out, and he carried this weight of guilt with him into adulthood.

His inner burden led to his chronic pessimism and depression, as well as to his looking physically as though he were carrying the weight of the world. Each of his relationships with women had been destroyed by his constant depressive outlook, leaving him feeling even more as though there was something inherently unworthy about him, and leaving him even lonelier.

Drinking, for Luke, was initially a conscious choice to lighten his burden. He felt less depressed for a few hours when he drank, and this in itself seemed a sufficient explanation for why he returned to drinking again and again. He was not aware that his use of alcohol soon moved beyond a rational choice, and became an addiction. If his drinking had indeed only been a conscious, practical decision, then knowing the trouble it caused his relationships, and the remorse he felt when unable to stop, he would have put an end to it. As you probably figured out, Luke's addiction was a response to the lifelong burden of his unworthiness and guilt. He drank to have some relief, as he said, but he was aware only of the direct relief it provided from his depressed feelings. He was not aware that he drank to reverse the feeling of helplessness underlying the impossible trap he lived in day-to-day. In this trap, having things for himself meant a fresh reason to feel guilty for being spoiled. When he drank he finally gave something to himself, expressing his lifelong rage at living in this guilty trap.

2. *What defenses kept Luke from seeing the key moment?*
For all his high intelligence, Luke was not an introspective man.

When he was most depressed, he responded by working harder, just as he had done as a child. This was a major defense. Underlying it, and outside his awareness, was the thought that if he worked hard enough, maybe he could finally prove that he was worthy of what he'd been given in life.

Besides his compulsive working, Luke had another defense: he avoided relying on others. In refusing outside help, he was again trying to avoid feeling guilty for expecting to receive more from others.

With these defenses in place, Luke was in no position to understand the underlying issues for which his addiction was a solution. Consequently, after he managed to stop drinking for a few weeks, he was shocked to see his drinking resume. Hard work had enabled him to accomplish so much in his life. He truly believed that as long as he buckled down it would be enough to deal with his alcoholism. When the key moment on his path to addiction arrived, therefore, he was unable to recognize it, or to use it to explore the drive behind his addiction in a thoughtful way.

3. What was the key moment on Luke's path to addiction?

The key moment in this episode was when Luke returned to his office after speaking with the chief. That was when the thought of drinking first entered his mind, though he subsequently worked all day and didn't start drinking until he arrived home.

4. What more direct actions could Luke have taken in place of the addictive act?

The event that precipitated Luke's key moment—his promotion—was not something he could do much to alter on his own, in a simple, practical way. As in many of the cases we've seen, what was important here was what the event *meant* to him. The best thing he could have done was to focus on that. What feelings were aroused in him by this offer? Did these feelings remind him of anything else in his life? Luke had never thought about his life in psychological terms, but he could have started then. Paying attention to these questions would have likely brought to mind his past experiences with receiving gifts and honors. He would then have seen this promotion as yet another honor, and remembered that he never felt worthy of such things. Once he saw that the present circumstance was just another instance of his old problem, he would have been able to separate some of his strong feelings from it. He could have said to himself, "I've always felt guilty about this sort of thing. That's been a big problem for me. I can see that being appointed acting chief is bringing up that issue. But if this is just part of a pattern, it means that this particular event can't be the real problem. It must be that it's just reviving something from my past." Having refocused his attention, he had a chance to avoid being overwhelmed by this new honor.

Thinking through what he was feeling was the most important thing Luke could do. But there were also some practical actions that would have helped him manage his helplessness trap. He could have called the chief and told him he needed a few days to think it over. This would have removed some of the pressure he felt in the moment and given him a chance to explore his reaction in more comfort. He also could have turned to someone else to talk about how he felt in order to help clarify his reaction. Of course, doing that would have conflicted with his defensive privacy, his avoidance of seeking help (just as he had ignored his friend's suggestion that he see a therapist, which would have been a good idea). So talking with another person would not have been easy for Luke. But as he recognized the issues behind his addiction, he might well have felt less guilty about asking for help.

ERICA

Erica hurried around her apartment getting ready to go out to meet her friend Jamie for a walk and talk in the park near Erica's house. She was in a good mood after the date she had with a new man last night. He was smart and seemed like a good listener, unlike most of the men she'd dated. He was also good-looking, and that didn't hurt. She had not had a real date for a couple of months. She finished getting dressed and went out to the entrance to the park where she could see Jamie was already waiting.

JAMIE: Hey, what's up? You look great, and happy.
ERICA: Hi! Yes, I guess I am.

The women began to walk up the path into the park. It was a beautiful spring day and new leaves were on the trees. They commented on the park for a few minutes before Jamie said to Erica that she looked like she had lost some weight. It was something they could talk about since Erica had long ago confided in Jamie about her problem of bingeing on food. At twenty-six years old, Erica felt it was particularly important to have a trim figure.

ERICA: Yes, I have lost some. It's one of the things I'm happy about. Since I broke up with Alex two months ago I haven't binged even once.
JAMIE: That's great. I guess it was good to get away from him.
ERICA: Yes. You were right to tell me to get out.

They walked a little more before Jamie spoke next. Erica had told her she was going to have a date with someone new last night.

JAMIE: So losing weight is just one of the things you're happy about? What else? Is it the new guy?

ERICA: Yes, he seems really nice.

JAMIE: You have to tell me all about it. I hope this one turns out better than the last, oh, several hundred.

ERICA: Come on. You know perfectly well I've had a grand total of three serious relationships. That's all.

JAMIE: Okay, but they've all been exactly the same.

ERICA: They have not. Okay, the first two were jerks, but Alex was good, for a while.

JAMIE: Erica! Sometimes you worry me. By "a while" don't you mean about three months?

ERICA: He was fine for about a year.

JAMIE (shaking her head): So, when he started to talk to you as if you were an idiot and left you to talk with other women at parties, which began pretty much the summer you met, that was "fine"?

Erica shrugged, and the friends walked in silence for a minute.

JAMIE: Look, you know that things were pretty bad for a long time before you finally broke up with Alex.

ERICA: Yes, okay, I know.

JAMIE: So what I'm saying is just the same as what we talked about when you broke up with him. You have to be careful. I'm not saying anything about this new guy. I haven't even given you a chance to tell me more about him! But you're one of those women, you know, and I don't want to see you hurt again.

ERICA: One of what women?

JAMIE: Those women who find men who treat them badly, then stay with them even though they're abusive.

ERICA: I know you said that to me when I broke up with Alex. I was upset then, so I agreed with you. But I don't know now. I don't think I'm like those women. I just made

a few bad choices. It isn't as though I like to be treated
badly.

JAMIE: I know that. But you have to admit your track record
is not good.

ERICA (*after a short pause*): No, I suppose it isn't.

JAMIE: So just be careful. Now, tell me about this new guy.

Two months went by, and Erica was still seeing the "new guy,"
whose name was Tim. Jamie had badgered Erica to keep her up-
to-date on how things were going between them so she could keep
a watchful eye out for what she said was Erica's "problem." Erica
went along with this partly because Jamie was her best friend and
partly because she worried that she might be right.

Things had gone okay with Tim, Erica thought, though his
attentiveness had been less than what it first appeared to be when
they met, and he had maybe seemed self-centered and a little cav-
alier in his treatment of her, at times. Jamie had reacted strongly
to hearing about those times, warning Erica that she was in her
usual mode again. Erica didn't see it that way. She was glad to be
with a new boyfriend, and if she was willing to put up with some
of his foibles, well, what was wrong with that?

She was out having dinner with Tim when he said he wanted
to ask her something.

TIM: Listen, I'm going to have a party to watch the basketball
finals at my place on Friday. There are going to be about
twenty guys coming over. People are driving in groups but
there aren't enough cars for everyone, so somebody has to
pick up a couple of the guys who live about twenty miles
out. It's around forty-five minutes to get there. Well, forty-
five minutes there and another forty-five minutes back
after the game. I can't do it because I have to be home,
manning the home front. I was thinking you might be able

to pick up the guys for me and maybe bring them home later.

ERICA (*startled*): This Friday?

TIM: Yes, it's the first game of the finals.

ERICA: I don't see . . . I mean, why can't one of the guys pick up the other guys?

TIM: I told you, there aren't enough cars. We're going to have eighteen guys in four cars, and some of those are little sports cars.

ERICA: Forty-five minutes is a long way. And you're talking about driving them back after the game?

TIM: Yes. We've got exactly the same problem taking them home as getting them here. I'll be cleaning up the mess at home, so I can't do it.

ERICA: Well, I don't know. I was hoping we could just go out Friday night together.

TIM: It's the finals! I've got this all planned out.

ERICA: What will I do while you and your friends are watching the game?

TIM: You can watch with us! The guys will be glad you're there.

ERICA: I don't like basketball. You know that. So, you're saying I'm just going to have to read a book in another room at your place, and try to keep out the noise?

TIME: You can do that, or you could go out somewhere.

ERICA: I don't know.

TIM: Look, I know it's a hassle, but it would mean a lot if you would help.

ERICA (*after a pause*): Okay.

They finished dinner with no more reference to the basketball plans. Erica felt uneasy. When the waiter asked if they wanted dessert she had a hard time saying no, though it had been her policy for a long time to avoid desserts. She and Tim had each come from work and were not staying together that evening, so Erica drove home alone. When she arrived she began looking through her kitchen cabinets. Since she had been watching her weight, there wasn't much there but an unopened box of crackers, a loaf of bread, and a box of spaghetti. She paused a moment. Her bingeing had stopped and her weight was down. "Oh, screw that!" she cried as she grabbed and flung open the box of crackers and began to eat one after another. At the same time she put water on to boil. By the time it was ready for the spaghetti she had finished the cracker box and was eating the bread with some peanut butter she'd found. The spaghetti wouldn't take very long now, she knew, even though she'd thrown in the entire box.

Growing up with her parents and two older brothers might have made Erica special as the only girl. But she was not. While she was eager to join in with her bigger brothers, who were each just a few years apart, the result was that she was assigned the lowest rank in every game. If it was spacemen, her brothers were the captain (sometimes the emperor) and the lieutenant, while she was the junior cadet. If it was playing forts, they were the general and the major and she was the private, given orders but neither authority nor respect. Her eagerness to join with them made her willing to put up with whatever indignity was required. Her father might have provided some relief if he had had an extra special place in his heart for his little girl, but he was more drawn toward his sons, whose energy and even wildness gave him a sense of pride. When all the children were around, his attention was almost always on the boys. Erica kept trying her best to draw his interest, but her efforts led to little more than a nod, and sometimes not even that. Indeed, it was his attitude toward her that the boys had picked up early on, and became the model for their disparaging treatment of their sister. Erica's mother would have been her salvation, but she was a quiet woman who also privately reveled in her sons' unruly behavior. Counting her brothers and her parents, then (even though her parents would have vehemently denied it), everyone in Erica's family saw the boys as far more valuable than her.

Erica felt that, of course. Even when she was small, she could sense that her position in the family was low, and though she would not have been able to give her feeling a name, it was shame. Like all small children, she had no context outside her family to understand her situation. All she knew was that she wanted to be included, and she had to do whatever she had to do to achieve that, even if only for a short time. Later in her life, when she found herself in a subordinate role in relationships, she interpreted that as just more evidence of her inferiority, another reason to feel ashamed.

ANSWERS TO DISCUSSION QUESTIONS

1. What are the underlying emotional themes that lead to Erica's experience of helplessness and, in turn, its addictive solution?

No doubt you saw the connection between Erica's experiences of shame and devaluation as a child and her later experiences with men as an adult. Her friend Jamie was right about her being one of "those women" who select abusive men. The reasons for this ruinous behavior are actually not limited to women. Usually, the basis for it is just what it was for Erica.

Erica had an impossible dilemma as a child. She had a normal need to be attached to, be loved by, and be cared about by the major people in her life—her parents and, to a lesser extent, her siblings. But these people she most needed were in reality uncaring and devaluing—even abusive. Children in Erica's position commonly solve this problem by bending themselves to fit with the people they need. In response to parents' dominating and belittling them, children adapt by being submissive and meek. When they grow up, this issue is often still very much alive in them and, without being fully aware of why they are doing it, they seek new people who are emotionally like the parents whose valuing and attention they had been seeking their whole lives. Unintentionally, then, they repeat the same sorts of devaluing relationships they had as children. Behind this need for attachment to hurtful people is often also a conviction in these children when they grow up that their own feelings are not worth caring about. The thought that commonly follows from this is, "If I stood up for myself, nobody would want to be with me."

As you have probably seen, the relationship between Erica's history and her food binges fits exactly with everything we know about addiction, and the drive behind addiction. When Erica felt she had to go along with Tim's unreasonable demands to chauffeur for his friends, she was back in her old devalued and ashamed trap. She had never been good at expressing her feelings about the way she was treated, for the reasons we saw just above: in her view she would have risked losing her relationship with Tim, and she wasn't worth fighting for anyway. But it would have been impossible for her not to be furious at some level. When she binged, she expressed her deep rage at the lifelong helplessness of her demeaned and subservient position ("Oh, screw that!" she'd said), while reversing that helplessness in the displaced act of compulsively eating.

2. What defenses kept Erica from seeing the key moment?

Throughout her life, Erica had found it hard to grasp the basis for her troubled relationships and her compulsive eating, despite her friend Jamie's best efforts to be helpful and give her good advice. Erica rationalized her symptoms as just bad choices. When Jamie pressed her about being one of those women who stay with abusive men, Erica's response was based on rational but superficial thinking. Erica had said, "It isn't as though I like to be treated badly," but this answer missed the point. Certainly Erica didn't like to be treated badly. But that could not explain why she, nonetheless, kept finding herself in situations where that was just the case. Erica avoided this kind of introspection, no doubt because it was a tender area for her. If she thought too much about putting herself in these debasing relationships she would feel even more ashamed, and would have to experience her sadness and anger at her lifelong devaluation. The same problem arose in thinking about her food addiction. She focused on losing weight to look better, rather than on the hopelessness and shame that led to her urge to eat.

3. What was the key moment on Erica's path to addiction?

Erica's key moment occurred when she had trouble not ordering a dessert. That was the first moment when the focus of her addiction—food—came to mind; though as usual it was quite a bit later that she carried out her addictive act. Even before the key moment, earlier during the meal when she felt uneasy about taking on the role of chauffeur, we can see that Erica was starting along the path to her addiction. This was the first point at which she began to feel trapped. It was an early signal to us that she was now on the path to her addiction. Unfortunately, this moment was not visible to Erica. If she had been more attuned to what was happening within her, she surely would have picked up this earlier sign that she was heading toward a binge, even before she had the conscious urge to eat the dessert.

In fact, if Erica had been in touch with the issues underlying her addiction, she could have prevented this binge long before the night of her meal with Tim, back when she first began to notice that her new boyfriend was acting like all of her old boyfriends. She would have recognized that she was embarking on the same old path that, if not cut short, would lead to the same hurt and enraged feelings, and the same addictive response.

4. What more direct actions could Erica have taken in place of the addictive act?

At the dinner, Erica was faced with a specific decision—a concrete choice of what action to take. One action—agreeing to drive Tim's friends to and from the game—led predictably to her addiction. The other choice—refusing to do this—would have taken her off that path. Of course, we know that just because the better choice is plain to see doesn't mean it's easy to act on. Behind Erica's compliance, after all, was the entire history and force of her need to hold on to relationships with hurtful people.

However, as we've seen, being aware of what is at stake in these key moments—control of your addiction—can be a helpful boost to taking an action to block it. And, as we've seen before, it was not necessary for Erica to make the best possible choice under the circumstances. She only needed to come up with something that was good enough to deal with her trap. If she couldn't bring herself to out-and-out refuse Tim's request, a lot of other partial solutions were available to her. She could have agreed to do only part of the task, for instance picking up some of the friends so they would arrive on time for the game, but leaving it to them to make a couple of trips home at the end of the night, when there was no time crunch. Or she could have offered to bring some of his friends who lived closest rather than the ones who lived farthest away, creating enough room in the cars for others to pick up the more distant people. Or she might have said she would help clean up at the end of the night so Tim could drive his friends home. Any of these and many other ideas might have come to her mind and eased her sense of helplessness enough to prevent her binge, even if she could not bring herself to take the most direct possible action.

BILL

In seventeen years of marriage Bill had been involved in five extramarital affairs. Four of the women he had slept with worked in the same company as he did, and one was a woman who lived in the neighborhood. Bill's wife, Cindy, knew about none of these until the couple's fifteenth anniversary, when Bill, filled with remorse, confessed. That was followed by a separation that lasted four months, during which time Bill lived in a nearby motel room and saw their two young children initially several times each week, partly to share driving them to school in the morning since his wife worked out of the home. Bill also had the children over to his place on weekends at first, and then visited them more and more frequently at the couple's home during the week. Eventually, Cindy told him he could return home and Bill left the motel with an absolute resolve never to give in to what he saw as his weakness again.

Bill was not an extraordinary-looking man. He was neither tall nor short, fat nor thin, muscular nor delicate. He was very smart but had never been a standout in school or especially noted for his conversational ability. Yet, he had a way with women that would have been the envy of his friends if he had let them in on his secret life. Bill himself could not explain it except to say he was comfortable with women.

Part of Bill's trouble describing his prowess with women was that by the time he had been married seventeen years at age forty-one, he had nearly forgotten the hours he'd spent as a teenager deliberately practicing how to talk with girls. He had done this with the same intensity as his friends who were pumping iron in the gym to stay on the football team. And he kept up his efforts longer and harder than many of them. Only the boys with the biggest muscles could compare with the smoothly invisible level of skill that he had developed.

However, Bill was not simply a phony. His plan was never to take advantage of the many girls, and later women, with whom he developed relationships. He was considerate and thoughtful, which were traits that actually proved more important to keeping the affairs going than his amazing ability to start them up. But there were two reasons why each affair ended. The first was that Bill was, after all, married. Incredible though it may seem from his history, he loved his wife. Over the years he had told himself that if she didn't know about his affairs, they couldn't hurt her. But this meant that if he began to worry he would be discovered, he had to end the affair. The other reason his affairs ended was that each of the women he found were married, too. Their marriages didn't seem to matter to a few of them, but at least three women left when they thought they were about to be discovered, and one had gone further and told her husband she was having an affair, thereby abruptly ending it.

That Bill loved his wife was the main reason she took him back. After fifteen years she knew that about him, despite what he had done.

For the next year the family healed and Bill was glad. He did still have thoughts of flirting with some of the attractive younger women at his office, but he held himself in check.

Bill was in charge of roughly one half of a highly successful software company, a business he had helped found in his early twenties in the midst of a high-tech boom. While several of his partners were in charge of marketing and sales, he was one of two programming whizzes who created the company's main products, then later ran teams of programmers to build upon them. He privately thought of himself as like his old friends who had been on the football team in high school and college—a big man on campus. Like them, his ability on his turf made him the star everyone on his team looked to for strength and leadership.

Lately, though, the company had been faltering. There was

new competition for their product line and they had struggled to stay ahead in development. A particular problem for Bill was that he and his cofounder and co-whiz, Isaac, ran separate divisions and Isaac's group had been doing better. Their updates and new products had captured both market share and attention from industry magazines. Bill's group had recently done neither.

It was Friday at noon and the company's leadership was having their monthly meeting to review the status of the business, something they had done more regularly since sales had declined over the past year. As each person spoke about his area there was tension in the room. Everyone understood that the challenges the company faced were inevitable in a rapidly growing field, but there was no way to ignore that it was Bill's division that was dragging them all down. They had danced around this for months. Partly, this was because Bill had repeatedly reassured them that his group was working hard to improve, and partly because Bill was clearly defensive and nobody felt comfortable being critical of him.

But today seemed like it would have to be different. Things were not going better and now one of the monthly magazines had written a damning review of the latest update from Bill's division. Bill had seen the review, of course, and had been first devastated, then enraged. Now, in the meeting, he was prepared for battle to protect his name and reputation, even if he was among colleagues and old friends.

The company president, also one of the original members of the firm, brought up the magazine review and said it would be a problem for them, not just for that product but because of the light it cast on the entire company. Bill immediately and angrily responded. The magazine had been unfair to measure this update against the newest version of their competitors'. He and his group had been working around the clock to get this out quickly and of course there would be flaws. Bill looked challengingly around the room. This time, people didn't shy away. Another partner asked why he had to work so quickly—why had they been so far behind that they needed to do a rush job now? Before Bill could answer the CFO spoke up. The company could ill afford to have another weak sales quarter, which would surely follow this poor review of one of their main products. Bill was outraged. He raised his voice a notch and began to talk about the successes he and his group had developed over the years. Looking straight at the CFO, he said that the company wouldn't have profits to lose if it had not been for his work. But then Isaac broke in. The men had been partners since the beginning of the company, and the mild rivalry that had developed between the two programming masters and their divisions had always been amiable. "I do think there is a problem here," Isaac began. "It's not just the latest update. The earlier versions lacked the power of our competitors. It won't be possible to bring this product up to the level of our competitors' without a rewrite of major parts of the system's core. Right now, it's like trying to make a bungalow into a mansion by giving it a new coat of paint."

Bill was beside himself. He felt like standing up and hitting Isaac. It wasn't just because of what Isaac said; it was that Bill couldn't deflect this criticism the way he could from everyone else in the room. Isaac was as brilliant and knowledgeable about programming as Bill, so telling him that he didn't know what he was talking about would have fallen flat, and Bill knew it. The best Bill could do was to say he knew there were some fixes that he and his group needed to make in their product, but he was absolutely sure they would be able to make them.

When the meeting broke up Bill returned to his office. He noted that his heart was still beating fast. He tried to do some work but had trouble concentrating. After an hour he was calmer but still upset. He left the office and walked down to the snack machines on the floor below. There was an attractive young woman there trying to choose which delectable to select from the candy machine. She worked in the company and Bill had seen her before, but they had never spoken. Bill introduced himself, though he knew that she knew who he was. He inquired about her process of deciding which candy to buy. She seemed a little flustered that one of the heads of the company was talking with her. They joked about the limited selection provided by the machine. Bill said that he would deal with that problem immediately, and she laughed. After a minute she said she had to get back to work, and Bill said he would walk her back to her desk and take the blame for her lateness with her boss, whom they both knew reported to Bill. By the time they parted Bill had arranged to meet her for a drink after work. Walking back to his own office, he was already thinking about where they might go after the drink, and how he could best word it when he called his wife to say he would be home very late.

Bill was an only child. His parents had a troubled marriage dominated by his father's extramarital affairs. Bill's father, Charley, seemed larger than life. Highly successful as a real estate developer, Charley was not just physically large but took over the room with his booming voice, overbearing personality, and—to the dismay of many—large cigars. His wife, Abby, Bill's mother, acted like a sort of appendage to him. A good mother, however, she quietly raised the boy without complaining about her husband or his affairs, which she knew of. Charley's need to be bombastic led not only to his womanizing but also to his mocking his son's abilities. "Nice try, little one," his father would say sarcastically when Bill tried to emulate his father's behavior. Bill was repeatedly crushed by his father's inability to grasp the boy's need to identify with him. Abby saw this clearly and tried to help by including Bill in her pursuits in art and design. As much as Bill loved and relied on his mother, he had also picked up his father's attitude toward her. Consequently, as he grew older, he came to chafe under, and reject, his mother's attention: being allied with her meant being further alienated from his father, and suffering further humiliation at his hands.

When Bill started dating, he entered a world he had often heard his father talk about, generally in relation to his father's self-proclaimed prowess. Even beyond the normal drives of development, therefore, it was important to Bill to compete in this area. While not physically imposing like his father, Bill used his intelligence and humor to attract and seduce women. At the same time, his deep love for his mother provided the genuine attachment that underlay his more superficial capacities to engage with women.

ANSWERS TO DISCUSSION QUESTIONS

1. What are the underlying emotional themes that led to Bill's experience of helplessness and, in turn, its addictive solution?

Growing up, Bill had been unable to identify in a positive way with his hypermasculine father. Charley's need to be more than others, a larger-than-life man, meant that he also needed to keep Bill small. Bill grew up, therefore, harboring painful doubts about his manhood and feeling overwhelmed and intolerably helpless when it seemed to him these doubts were being validated. So it was important to Bill, later in life, to think of himself as a big man on campus and to associate with the physically big athletes on the football team. For Bill, the ability to attract and seduce women became especially important, and even more valuable, to him over the years, because he had been so expert at it from an early age, thanks to his tremendous motivation. Because his inner doubts about his masculinity were lifelong, Bill's need to seduce women was ongoing. And with the strength of this need behind it, Bill's womanizing became an addiction. Not surprisingly, this addiction was especially powerful when Bill felt weak. On those occasions, the old trap of feeling the smallest and least "manly" was evoked in his mind, enraging him and impelling him to reverse his helplessness by exercising his ability to attract women.

The women Bill sought were not chosen at random. And it was not a coincidence that all of Bill's longer affairs were with married women. The explanation for this lies behind another facet of Bill's early life. His father's failure to bond with Bill disrupted Bill's development through one of the normal phases of early childhood, when very young boys dream of having their mothers for themselves. In the ordinary course of development, this phase ends. But for Bill, whose profound disconnection and anger toward his father remained central to his being, besting his father in his dealings with the opposite sex was critical. It was one thing to be able to prove his masculinity by seducing women. But to win them away from their husbands was the best of all worlds. He conquered not only the women, but defeated his male rivals, their husbands, as well. As a way to reverse feelings of intolerable helplessness, it was a near-perfect addictive solution.

2. What defenses kept Bill from seeing the key moment?

Bill was another person who had focused on his behavior but not its nature or causes. When he finally confessed his affairs to his wife he saw them as failures to behave properly and a weakness of his personality. He gave no thought to why he was driven to have these affairs, or even if there was a reason for them. When he began to think of seducing another woman after the confrontational meeting in the story, he had nothing to slow him on his path except fleeting thoughts of having sworn never to do that again. Unfortunately, those could not measure up to the old power behind his addictive drive. With no understanding of what was happening within his mind or how he could deal with it, he could not stop the process from continuing to its end.

Bill's automatic, defensive response, when challenged, itself posed another problem. He could not hear or accept criticism without feeling that it was a blow to his manhood. That made it impossible for him to think clearly about what emotions this latest crisis had stirred up in him.

3. What was the key moment on Bill's path to addiction?

The first moment Bill thought about approaching another woman was when he saw her at the snack machine. But as usual we could look back further to precursors of the key moment. Bill's reaction at the meeting was an example. Though not the key moment, this was when Bill deployed his defense of "fighting back." If he had been attuned to his defensive style, his eruption at the meeting would have sent up a red flag. He could have recognized that something was being stirred up in him, something that was emotionally important. With this awareness he could have recognized that his addiction might be around the corner. In fact, if he had known himself and how his addiction worked, he could have recognized, way back when his division first started performing poorly, that he was vulnerable to his addiction. He might have seen that he was in a familiar position, his power and ability challenged. He might have seen, ahead, the old trap closing in on him.

4. What more direct actions could Bill have taken in place of the addictive act?

In Bill's mind he was facing an intolerable challenge to his manhood. In the aftermath of the meeting, he was unable to concentrate, and real strategies for dealing with the situation at hand were clouded by his rage. If Bill could have stepped back and seen himself in the throes of his old helplessness trap, his internal monologue would have sounded something like this: "Well, here I am again feeling like I'm being beaten down by my father and that I absolutely have to fight to preserve my self-worth as a man. But what's really happening here is that the company wants better products from me and my people. That's a big problem. But it's not the really big, enraging, problem of having to prove that I'm a man."

Even if Bill couldn't think through the issues so clearly, and he was unable to dissipate his rage by putting it where it belonged—in his past—he still had many more direct actions he could have taken. He was furious with Isaac, but he could have gone to him after the meeting and talked to him. He and Isaac had known each other and been partners for a long time. Bill could have told Isaac that he didn't appreciate his undercutting remarks in the meeting. He could have said that if Isaac had an opinion about his or his group's work he should come to Bill about it, not attack him in an open meeting. He could also have talked with the CFO and others at the meeting, with a similar message. He didn't like being blindsided or ganged up on.

He could also have acted more directly against his sense of helplessness by drafting a memo to the partners. This would give Bill the chance to shape his argument from the meeting and show them how much he and his group had contributed over the years. He might have added that he was more aware and better prepared to handle the current problems than colleagues outside his area of expertise and—given his long and successful career—they had good reason to maintain their confidence in him.

Had Bill taken any of these steps, it is likely that his compulsion to repeat his addiction would have sharply decreased. And, of course, if he had recognized the deep threat he had felt much earlier as his division began to fall behind competitors, he might have avoided the final struggle with his addiction altogether.

PART III

Living with Someone
Who Has an Addiction

Everything we've discovered about the nature of addiction is important to understand if you live with someone who has an addiction. A helpful approach does not mean acting as a therapist for a loved one. But if you understand addiction—and the many myths and common mistakes that have shaped our treatment of addiction—then you are in a much better position to deal with the problems that addictions produce in relationships.

POPULAR IDEAS ABOUT LIVING WITH A PERSON WITH ADDICTION: DO THEY MAKE SENSE?

Now that we have seen addiction in a new way, we can critically reexamine some popular ideas about it.

"TOUGH LOVE"

Let's begin with some general observations. If addiction were viewed as a kind of bad habit or a moral weakness, then it might make sense to be tough on the person who has the problem. After all, sometimes if people seem to be lazy or unfocused it can be helpful to give them a kick in the pants, or set limits on their behavior so they'll shape up. One way to do this is to avoid or ignore the person until he or she gets the message to change his behavior. But does this thinking apply to addiction?

We know that addiction is not a bad habit or a moral weakness or laziness or the result of being unfocused. It is psychologically identical to other compulsive behaviors that are not usually thought of as addictions, such as having to compulsively clean your house, exercise, or shop. It is an emotionally driven symptom, a particular way to manage difficult feelings as I have described. Nobody suggests that behaviors like compulsively cleaning your house be treated by being tough on the person doing the cleaning, or ignoring them until they stop. Why do people suggest these ideas for addiction?

Ultimately, this is because the psychological nature and mechanism of addiction have not been understood. But the particularly judgmental view of addictions that has been prevalent throughout human history has clearly been a reaction to their harmful effects on others.

When people engage in compulsive activities like excessively cleaning their houses, they generally don't cause harm or pain to those around them. As a consequence, it is easy to empathize with these people, to see their suffering and to be drawn toward them to help, rather than away from them with disdain. But when a person's behavior is harmful or painful to those around them, he or she is often consciously or unconsciously viewed as self-centered, thoughtless, and immoral. This view is reinforced by the fact that the behavior continues despite the harm it causes others. Under these circumstances, it is easy to fall into righteous anger. The thought process goes something like this: "I understand that addiction is a problem that is hard to deal with. But problem or not, she is hurting the people around her—people she's supposed to care about, people who depend on her. In the end, it doesn't really matter how hard it is to deal with. She just shouldn't be doing this to the people she loves."

Once this thought has set in it's hard to maintain a calm and neutral perspective toward either the person in question or the problem from which he or she suffers. It begins to seem reasonable and fair to treat the person as though she is bad. Being tough therefore seems like a rational approach.

A related tendency—if you don't understand the nature of addiction and are filled with frustration and anger—is to treat the addicted person as not only bad, but also dumb: "I've talked to him over and over, but he's too stupid to get it through his thick head what he's doing to himself and others."

It is easy to empathize with these reactions. Living with a person with addiction is very often frustrating, angering, sad, and depressing. But these reactions are not a good basis for dealing with your loved ones, or with the problem they are facing. The first step in dealing with someone suffering with addiction is to understand for yourself how addiction works. This can help you avoid suffering the extra pain of misinterpreting what the addiction means about your relationship. From there, you can think through what is really happening between the two of you.

As you thoughtfully approach your relationship, there is one other critical thing to keep in mind. *It is absolutely essential that you take care of yourself, for both your own sake and that of your partner.* This is very different from being tough on your partner. Here is an example:

Ian and Anna

Ian and Anna lived with their two children—Jesse, age nine, and Kaitlyn, age seven months—in an apartment house downtown. Anna had been drinking heavily for the past half year, starting soon after the birth of their daughter. When their son, Jesse, had started kindergarten, and before Kaitlyn's birth, both parents had worked full-time; with Jesse in school Anna had been able to return to her career as a bank branch manager. But the birth of Kaitlyn meant Anna needed to be at home again. The family was financially stressed because of losing Anna's income at the same time they had new expenses for the baby. But the bigger problem for Anna was that she loved her work. She had given it up with much regret when Jesse was born, but there had been no choice about this since Ian was able to make much more money than she could. It had to be her career that was postponed. Now the crisis had recurred. Although both parents loved their new child, the fact was that Kaitlyn had not been planned, and for Anna the new arrival felt like a crushing burden. When Kaitlyn was two months old, Anna began to drink.

When Anna drank she became irritable and distracted. She attended to the baby just enough to be sure she was fed and changed, but Anna was often content to place the child in a playpen with a mobile and some stuffed toys while she lounged on the sofa drinking and watching television. Ian knew she had been drinking as soon as he came home, and was deeply upset by it. But he was just as disturbed by the confusion and disappointment he could see in the eyes of Jesse, who had always been close to his mother. Over several months Ian told Anna that her behavior in the house simply could not continue. He emphasized not just her poor care for their baby but the pain she was causing Jesse. When she was not drinking, Anna always said she was very sorry, and clearly she was. She tried to patch it up with her son by spending extra time with him, helping with his homework, and making special foods she knew were his favorites. When she was sober she closely tended to Kaitlyn.

But the pattern continued, and before long Ian told Anna that if she was going to drink he was going to hire a babysitter to stay with her and the baby while he was at work. Anna was insulted and furious at this idea. Ian understood how she felt and was saddened by it. It was one reason he had been reluctant to confront her with this ultimatum before now. But at this point he could see no choice, for the sake of the entire family. He also made it clear to Anna that they could no longer all live together as things were going. He would have to consider telling her to go live with her mother while he and a babysitter managed by themselves. Her days of being drunk at home had to end.

Anna, too, felt backed into a corner at this point. She felt unable to stop drinking, but she was not going to lose her family over her drinking at home. So every day that she drank, which was still most days, she left her baby with the sitter Ian had hired and did her drinking in a nearby restaurant.

Ian's ultimatum did not help Anna stop drinking any more than she had been able to stop on her own. And, as much as she was unavailable to her baby and to Jesse when she had been drinking at home, now she was away from them even more. This was very sad for all of them. But it was not sadder than the destructiveness of her drinking in front of her children. Ian had taken an appropriate action. He was not intentionally being "tough" on Anna; toughness had nothing to do with it. He was protecting himself and his children. And he was also protecting Anna. It was far better for her to see her son and baby when she was sober than for her to create scenes in the house that diminished her in her children's eyes and added tension to the entire family.

Setting limits is a reasonable response to dangerous (including emotionally hurtful) situations. It should be motivated by the need to protect yourself and your family, not as a prod or punishment for the person with addiction. Being tough or punishing has no place in treating addiction, but protecting yourself always makes sense.

"Enabling"

The "enabling" idea is that if you help a person with addiction avoid negative consequences of his or her behavior then you are enabling—allowing or encouraging—the addiction. Here is a common example.

John is a man with alcoholism. Sometimes he drinks so much that he oversleeps the next morning. His job would be in jeopardy if his boss knew this was why he didn't show up some days, so his wife Ellen regularly calls his work to say he is sick. Ellen's friend tells her to stop doing this because she is enabling his alcoholism by preventing its consequences—in this case, the loss of John's job. Is Ellen's friend right?

In order to think about this, we just need to know one thing: enabling is basically the *opposite* of tough love.

Tough love is based on the idea that addiction can be improved by being hard on the person with the behavior. This does not make sense because if adverse consequences could stop addiction, nobody would have an addiction. The drive behind addiction is simply not affected by adverse consequences, as we know. Doing the opposite of tough love—helping to avoid adverse consequences—is just as unhelpful, and for the same reason. The drive behind addiction is also not affected by the absence of consequences. When Ellen calls in sick for John she is not doing his addiction any good. But if she stopped calling in sick for him she would not be doing his addiction any good, either. Given this, what should she do?

Figuring out the most sensible behavior for the partner or family of a person with addiction is not a black-or-white matter. For example, sometimes a degree of withdrawal from the person with addiction does make sense—not as a punishment, but because it is a way to communicate the seriousness of the situation. There are times when it is helpful for a family, or individual family members, to tell a loved one that they will not see him or talk with him as long as his addictive behavior persists. When this works well it is because the limit being set is heard in a different way than words. People often respond to actions more than words, not just because the actions have unwanted effects, but also because words have been tuned out and discounted. Taking an action can have the effect of startling someone into a different perspective on himself. Again, this has nothing to do with being tough or trying to punish someone. It is just thoughtful limit-setting made necessary when words have proved inadequate for communicating your message.

The same reasoning applies to enabling. Whether Ellen should call in sick for her husband, John, is not a black-or-white matter. If we believed that John would be able to see the seriousness of his addiction more clearly as a result, then we might encourage Ellen to stop calling in for him. This experiment would not take long. John, now on probation at work, would either be impelled into a new perspective, or he would not. If his outlook changed, then he might be able to alter his behavior enough to keep his job, though this would not mean, of course, that his addiction was cured. John might be able to change the pattern of his drinking just enough to get into work on time, without cutting down in any significant way.

If Ellen stopped calling in for John, and he still did not change his drinking pattern, then Ellen would have to make some hard choices. These would be based on achieving the best results for her, John, and their family. In any case, they should not depend on a rule that she *should* stop calling in because to do so would enable him.

For example, what if Ellen resumed calling in sick for John and as a result she preserved his job, and with it the family's income? That might be the best choice for now. While covering for John or not covering for him might both be irrelevant to his addiction, at least this way the family would be financially protected for the time being. This would also buy time for Ellen to consider other decisions about living with John, perhaps setting other forms of limits or, best of all, creating enough time to allow John to get help with his addiction. This could range from urging him to read this book, to having a professional consultation, to arranging an ongoing outpatient therapy, to exploring inpatient treatment. Ellen could also make an appointment to speak with a professional herself about her situation, something that is often very helpful.

The bottom line is that any decision about enabling ought not to be made rigidly. Just as people are all different, so are relationships and the situations in which people find themselves. Each circumstance should be thought through on its own merits. This is particularly true for children and adolescents, as I will explain at the end of this chapter. First, let's look in more general terms at relationships between adults.

ADDICTION IN ADULT RELATIONSHIPS

When people live together they influence each other in ways that are both obvious and not so obvious. Over time, in any relationship, both people change. Sometimes this is wonderful. When two people love each other they gradually become more sensitive to each other's deepest wishes and fears, allowing them to provide each other with a life that is as happy and meaningful, and as free from unnecessary pain, as possible. But the same mutually adaptive changes occur when either or both members of the relationship have emotional issues and symptoms, such as addictions, to which the other person must adapt. The original problem, addiction in this case, leads to many other difficulties that may be even more destructive than the addiction itself. The most common damages to the relationship beyond the addictive behavior itself are the loss of love, trust, and self-esteem of both members.

Consider a husband who suffers with alcoholism. We know that his drinking is a response to overwhelming feelings of helplessness that arise inside of him. We also know that certain kinds of circumstances or events will arouse old issues within him that lead to those helpless feelings, and then to their addictive solution. We understand that his drinking is emotionally compelled by this inner mechanism and that it has nothing inherently to do with his caring or love for those around him. And we know that once the episode has passed, he may well be filled with not only shame because he has been unable to control his behavior, but also guilt because he has injured those he loves, and a sense of despair because he has no idea what led him to repeat it.

But that is not the way his drinking feels to his spouse or his family. For them, his drinking is evidence that he is uncaring, irresponsible, and untrustworthy. If he really loved them, they think, he would stop. This view is often hardened by the fact that those living with the person with addiction have tried their best. Over a long period of time they have often been patient and caring. They have put up with a lot. But it hasn't seemed to matter. The person with the addiction repeats his or her behavior over and over. And since nobody can stay patient forever, eventually those living with him become convinced that they are dealing with someone who truly is unloving and unlovable. Like the person suffering with the addiction, they become trapped in their own anger and despair.

Below I will tell the stories of two couples whose relationships were torn apart by addiction. Then we will see how understanding the nature of addiction, as we've discussed in this book, can help them.

THE BRYANTS

Phyllis and Peter Bryant were married when they were twenty-five and twenty-six years old, respectively. They met in college, and when Peter went on to graduate school in environmental science in the same large city, Phyllis applied to the same university the following year in her field (English literature) so they could be together. When they were married a couple of years later, their friends said it was a match made in heaven. They shared interests, seemed to always want to be together, and were obviously in love.

Peter began to drink in college, but it was not a major problem then. He was able to make good grades, was never embarrassingly drunk at parties, and maintained close friendships. His drinking didn't interfere with his time with Phyllis, or their growing relationship. While Phyllis noticed his drinking, and once or twice questioned him about it, he brushed aside her questions. And since his drinking was not causing any real trouble, she shrugged it off. To the extent it remained on her mind, she thought it was a college thing that he would outgrow.

In graduate school Peter continued to drink, though not much differently than he had in college. He was one of those fortunate people whose education was in a field that he really cared about. As a result, his classes, no matter how difficult, were not a burden for him and he sailed through to his master's degree. Phyllis followed with her own master's the following year.

Peter managed to obtain a position studying water pollution, working in a smaller, more rural town. It was certainly a job in his field, and he believed it was important work, but his dream had been to study ecological systems more broadly. For the first time, he was doing something for which he lacked real passion. The couple's move to a small town was another adjustment, since they both loved the excitement and attractions of a big city. Phyllis was unable to find her ideal work in the new town, so she took a job as an administrative assistant.

Peter's drinking started to increase about six months after they arrived in their new home. He began to come home and open a beer, then another, before dinner. His drinking continued during the meal and usually afterward. When Phyllis talked with him about this, he said he was more tired doing this job than he had been all through college and graduate school. He said he needed a break at the end of the day.

Although she was concerned about his drinking, Phyllis felt she understood it. Peter had been disappointed with his work soon after the job began. She knew that he had hoped it would be more challenging. Before they moved he had talked hopefully about it, comparing it to a postgraduate course in a subspecialty area. Instead, he found the work repetitive and dull. So Phyllis saw his drinking as a product of this job stress and did her best to be supportive of him during this transition. If he needed to drink, then let him drink.

As time passed, Peter's drinking became worse. He drank in larger quantities and continued to drink through dinner. On other days, he ate quickly, and then sat on the couch drinking far into the night. When Phyllis tried to talk with him about it, he became testier. The more she pressed him the more he accused her of adding to his problems. Why couldn't she leave him alone? Couldn't she see he was unhappy? Drinking was the only way he could get through the day, he would say, before turning away and focusing on the television and his drink.

Phyllis was badly hurt by this. She tried to insist that he talk with her. "What do you mean that's the only way you can get through the day?" she cried. "You have a wife! You can talk to me if you have problems."

But the more she tried to shake Peter out of his increasing isolation, the more he seemed to withdraw. He began to stop coming home right after work. When he did show up, he was drunk. Phyllis was distraught. In her increasing desperation she shifted back and forth between trying to comfort Peter and shouting at him. When she was the most angry and frustrated she would tell him he'd changed; he wasn't the man she had married.

Peter wasn't drunk all the time. Sometimes he was genuinely sad and apologetic. He promised to stop drinking. He told her he loved her, and he meant it. He said he felt terrible about the way he was treating her, and he meant that, too. There were times he was like his old self. On one occasion her car got a flat during a snowstorm, leaving her stranded by the side of a remote road. She called Peter and he was there in record time despite the awful driving conditions. He changed the tire and slowly drove back in front of her because visibility had turned so bad that he insisted she follow him in case of fallen tree branches or stuck cars in the road. At times like that, and when Peter was apologetic about his drinking, Phyllis was more than willing to forgive him and tell him they'd make a new start. But then he would drink again, and Phyllis's ability to bounce back, to have hope that this time would be different, became weaker and weaker.

Things got worse. Peter began to lie about his drinking. When he came home late he tried to sneak into bed without waking her. In the morning he denied he had been drinking, saying he had come home late because he was working. Then Phyllis began to find the hidden bottles in the house. Peter had moved on from beer to vodka sometime before that and she found the small vodka "nip" bottles in the back of his closet, in his sock drawer, and in the garage behind the paint. At first Peter said he didn't know how they got there. Later, he said that they were old bottles, and that he had stopped drinking weeks ago and forgot those were still in the house. When he swore that the ones she had found were the last of them and she found more a week later, she had reached the end of her rope. She threw him out of the house and Peter moved into a motel room.

The couple was still living apart when Phyllis later talked with me about her marriage. She described the long, downhill course of Peter's drinking, the fights they'd had, the broken promises, the attempts to repair their relationship, and the repeated disappointments. After all of that, though, she said that the worst of it, the part she could never understand or live with, was Peter's lying. He had not just lied, she explained; he had lied repeatedly, consciously, to her face. "If it had only been his drinking I could have stood it," she said. "I married him for life, and to me that meant being with him and staying with him through whatever problems he had. But the lying was different. A marriage can't exist without trust." She thought a moment, and then added, "I tried to think of his lies as the drinking talking, but there were so many times he lied when he hadn't had anything to drink. Like when I found the vodka nips. He was stone sober when he told me that the bottles were old." She shook her head. "Alcoholism I can understand. I've heard enough about it to know that it's not something he can just stop at will. But the lying . . . I simply cannot understand why a person who loves someone can lie like that. I know that I cannot live with a man whom I can't trust."

Peter and Phyllis had loved each other, and that love had not completely died by the time they separated. Could the disastrous path of their marriage have been altered, even with Peter's addiction continuing as it had?

For Phyllis, the worst problem was not Peter's drinking, but his lying about it. It's often the case in relationships where one person has an addiction, that lying about the addiction—with its resultant destruction of trust—is the fatal problem. Looked at this way, the question of whether Phyllis and Peter's relationship could be saved became a question of whether something could be done about this loss of trust.

Peter's lies denied and distorted facts, but it was their meaning to Phyllis that made them so toxic. To her, Peter's lies meant that he was no longer treating her as his partner, his confidant, his companion in life. They meant he saw her as an outsider, some-one from whom he would conceal his inner and most intimate secrets. They meant, in short, that he no longer thought of her or related to her as his wife. To Phyllis, Peter's lies also meant that he was willing to manipulate her. This added insult to injury. It seemed that not only had Peter lost his connection to her, but also he was willing to belittle her.

Phyllis interpreted her husband's behavior as a sign that he no longer loved or respected her. But what was going on inside of Peter—what were his actual motivations for the way he was be-having?

When Peter began to drink more heavily, he was responding to old issues within himself that had been stimulated by his first job. He had loved most of his work in school and done well be-cause of that. This was especially fortunate for Peter because it had long been the case that whenever he thought he was being used or degraded, he felt helpless and enraged. In college he felt required courses outside his major were an unfair, "irrelevant" demand on him—and therefore demeaning. His heaviest drink-ing episodes in college were always related to those classes. As he completed these requirements, though, his drinking lessened and by the time he attended graduate school, his drinking caused few problems.

But Peter's new job was a different story. He quickly grasped its essentials, and then found it repetitive. Having to do it every day left him frustrated, just as his required courses in college had. It revived his sense that he was being used and demeaned. On top of that, this work did not have any definite end; there was no end of the semester to look forward to. His old trapped feeling returned and increased, and with it so did his drinking.

None of this had anything directly to do with Phyllis. She was badly hurt by his behavior but its cause and purpose had to do with Peter, not her. And Phyllis understood this. She said that as far as drinking went, she saw it as Peter's problem, and she was prepared to be there to help him work out his problems—whatever they were. But his lying was a different matter. That didn't seem to be just a problem within him. That seemed to be directly about his relationship with her and what she meant to him. Was she right? The answer to that question depends on why Peter lied.

Shame

Although he did not understand his addiction or its inner workings, Peter was not blind. He could see what was happening to him and he was ashamed about it. He could also see that he was hurting his wife—and felt awful about that too. He had proved to himself many times that he could not control his drinking, so he reasoned that the best way to protect his wife was to conceal it from her. What she didn't know couldn't hurt her. Later, when she found out the truth, he was filled with deep regret and promised to stop. He meant this when he said it but it was a promise he should not have made. By saying he would stop, he was making the same false assumption as those who think addiction is like a bad habit—something you can fix if you only try hard enough. Since he was unable to keep his promise, his guilt and shame increased. That meant that he needed to lie about his drinking that much more.

His lying itself was also a source of shame. Not only did he feel bad about it, but also Phyllis had made it clear that she hated it and was enraged about it. In the trap in which Peter was now living, that left only one solution. He would have to do a better job concealing the fact that he was lying. In effect, the more he lied the more he felt he had to lie.

His shame also led to more drinking. The original source of his addiction was a sense of being used and debased by others as if they were better than him. But his shame about drinking and failing to be able to stop and about lying were all further sources of feeling debased. A vicious cycle of drinking, lying, and shame was created, and soon it ran on its own. Like his drinking itself, although it led to his wife suffering terribly, it was essentially independent of his feelings about her. Phyllis's interpretation of Peter's lying as a sign that he no longer loved or respected her, though understandable, was not correct.

But this raises another question. Phyllis recognized early on that it was Peter's lying, more than his drinking, that she could not accept. And she let Peter know. "If only you would just tell me that you were drinking, or that you were thinking about drinking, I could help you!" she said repeatedly. "I want us to deal with this together. Let me in on it. I'd be a lot less mad if you told me you felt like you had to have a drink instead of lying to me about it."

If Peter's lying was not, at heart, about his relationship or his feelings about Phyllis, then why didn't he respond to her desperate appeals? Couldn't he see how important it was to her that he be honest, even if he did drink?

Partly, Peter seemed to be oblivious to his wife's pleas for the reason I described just above. He did hear Phyllis and did try to change. But when he could not stop drinking, his guilt and shame overran her good advice to be honest. Then his false reasoning kicked in: he could spare both her and himself from the pain of his failure to stop drinking and his failure to stop lying about it if he could just keep her from knowing the truth.

But there was another factor as well. Phyllis was sincere when she said she would be less angry with him if only he told her. However, it would have been almost impossible for her to not be angry and disappointed at all. And Peter was well aware of that and highly sensitive to it. Because of his own shame, he could not stand even a small amount of Phyllis's criticism. He could hear her only as confirming his most awful feelings about himself, leading him to try to avoid her.

Shame and guilt provide powerful reasons for lying in a relationship. Lying caused by these factors does not, in itself, mean that the person no longer loves or respects his partner.

Lying as a part of addiction

Another and even more basic reason that Peter lied has to do with the nature of addiction itself. We know that addictions are driven by a powerful, necessary drive to fight against overwhelming helplessness. We also know that factors that are part of the effort to reverse helplessness are driven by the same force as the final addictive act. For example, if someone tried to block Peter from entering a liquor store while he was heading for a drink, he would have been enraged and fought to get through—because getting into the store was just as driven as drinking. Likewise, if someone threatened Peter's drinking by attempting to reveal where he hid his vodka nips, he would have been furious and tried to stop him. It's the same situation for lying. When lying is protecting an addiction, it is just as driven as the addiction itself. This is why it persists despite its effects on others, even loved others. Its disastrous consequences are generally just an awful side effect, like the example I gave early in this book of a person breaking his wrist trying to get out of a cave where he is trapped. That person is not self-destructive; he is just overwhelmed by the need to battle overwhelming helplessness.

This, then, was another reason that Phyllis's interpretation of Peter's lying as a sign of his loss of love and respect for her was not right. This misinterpretation was especially sad and ironic for Phyllis, since she was much less hurt by Peter's drinking precisely because she knew it was a compulsive problem that arose within him. If only she could have seen that his lying was exactly the same as his drinking, just another part of the same addiction, she would not have been so hurt by it.

The actions that are part of an addictive process are impelled by the same powerful drive as the addictive act itself. Lies are common examples of this. When they are directly related to the addiction, they are no more a sign of general untrustworthiness than the addiction itself.

How to tell when lying is just an aspect of addiction

For spouses and family members of someone with addiction, it may seem difficult to understand whether a destructive defensive behavior like persistent lying should be treated as another symptom of the addiction or not. But, by looking closely at loved ones' behavior there is a simple way to test this. The Bryants' story offers a good example. When Phyllis was stuck in a snowstorm, Peter came to her rescue. He neither questioned her call for help nor hesitated to come to her. He put her safety ahead of his, not only by driving to her but then also driving in front so he would encounter any sudden obstacles; if there was going to be an accident it would affect him, not her.

This episode had little lasting meaning to Phyllis because Peter continued drinking and lying afterward. But it was important. Peter's actions that day showed that outside of his addiction, his love for her, his devotion to her, and his trustworthiness as a husband were all still alive. Phyllis discounted this evidence because it did not fit with the other instances in which Peter had been untrustworthy. She had not recognized the essential fact that those other incidents were all addiction-related.

There was other evidence of Peter's continued dedication to Phyllis, too. He often told Phyllis that he loved her. He often told her he would stop drinking precisely because he knew how devastating it was for her. Again, these moments were buried in his subsequent lying and broken promises. It was natural for Phyllis to lose track of the fact that when Peter said those things, he meant them. But by writing off his protestations of love, she placed herself in just the position she could not stand. She believed the awful idea that she really had lost her husband—that he was not the man she had married. His addiction, with its dishonesty and withdrawal, combined with her mistaken interpretation of what it all meant, had blinded her to the deeper reality of Peter's feelings.

The simple test for people living with those who have an addiction, then, is to ask the question: How do they behave in areas that are unconnected to the addiction? If your loved ones are honest and caring in ways that are independent of their addictive behavior, that's the best indication of their true feelings toward you.

How do you fix the relationship?

Needless to say, Phyllis had every right and reason to be angry and sad, and even to separate from Peter. It was emotionally healthy for her to protect herself in whatever way she felt best. But she also deserved to have a deeper understanding of what was happening between them, for her own sake as well as for the sake of their marriage. She deserved to see that her feelings were based on incorrect interpretations of Peter's actions—and incorrect in a way that caused her additional pain. If she had recognized that Peter's drinking and lying were simply two parts of the same problem within Peter, she would not have had to feel unloved, disrespected, and alone. She could have seen that although Peter's behavior had certainly changed, he was indeed still the same man she had married.

If Phyllis had realized this, the couple would have had a chance to de-escalate their destructive course. They could have built on those moments when Peter was acting like his old self, recognizing them as valid indicators of what they still had together. Talking together, they would have been in a good position to see past Peter's addiction to the problem behind the addiction. And working as a team, it would not have been hard for them to figure out what was happening with Peter and between them. His drinking worsened after he took a job that had revived old, intolerable feelings of being trapped. Quitting had seemed out of the question because it was Peter's very first job out of school and, in any case, he needed the work to support them. But if they could have talked about the way his job was affecting both him and their marriage, they might have decided together that it was better for him to quit. He might not have work for a while, but their marriage would survive. Indeed, their marriage might well be stronger for the fact that they had been able to work this out together. When Peter inevitably fell into his old trap in the future, he would be less ashamed to tell Phyllis about his feelings and his urges to drink, and she would be more able to deal with them without feeling personally abandoned.

THE BECKERS

Scott and Danielle Becker had been married for five tumultuous years. Scott had gambled away literally everything they had earned—and more—during their time together. He had twice been bailed out by his parents-in-law and owed them twenty-five thousand dollars. He had accumulated debt on three credit cards amounting to another twenty thousand dollars. Even if he were to stop gambling immediately and permanently, it would take years to pay off these debts. Understandably, Danielle was furious with Scott, and she was furious nearly all the time. She was angry about his ruining their finances. She was angry about his lying about gambling. She was angry at his secretiveness (he tried to hide his calls to his bookie, hide the fact he was following his sports bets on TV, and hide bank accounts he had opened on his own). But there was one more thing that angered and saddened her just as much as these things Scott had done: she felt that over the past few years, she herself had changed as a person, and she did not like the person she had become.

Scott and Danielle had been college sweethearts, and they married right after their graduation. They were living proof of the saying that opposites attract. Scott had always been moody and depressed. Danielle was calm and upbeat, always ready with a smile and a thoughtful word. She brightened his life. When she agreed to marry him, Scott knew he was the luckiest man in the world.

But now, five years later, Danielle had been transformed. Her face was drawn and she never seemed to smile. Her voice was raised, critical, even sarcastic. She was suspicious and guarded. And she hated being that way. As much as Scott wondered what had happened to the woman whose love of life had lifted his own, Danielle wondered about herself. They both knew that it was his gambling that had spoiled things. But that wasn't enough of an explanation for Danielle. She saw herself as a failure. She had always believed that people were just doing their best in life; everyone had flaws and everyone deserved compassion. She had known that Scott had troubles from the time she met him and had taken on his moodiness and depression with patience, seeing them as superficial blemishes cloaking a wonderful man underneath. Yet she seemed to have lost her empathy and compassion for him. She would not have believed that her personality could be so changed in such a short time, no matter what he did. She could only think there must be something wrong with her. So, beyond her fury, Danielle became depressed.

The Beckers' case offers another example of the way addictions can spoil relationships. While Phyllis Bryant was mainly upset that her husband no longer loved her, Danielle Becker suffered with the feeling that she was a bad wife because of her anger and criticisms of Scott. She sometimes even believed Scott when he told her that her negativity was making his gambling worse. Such self-recrimination is another corrosive by-product of addiction in relationships. And, like the belief that one is no longer loved, it is the result of not fully grasping the nature of addiction. Danielle and Scott needed to recognize a fundamental fact:

Because addiction is an internal problem arising from sources within the person who has an addiction, it cannot be the result of a partner's behavior.

Scott's blaming Danielle arose from his shame about his gambling. If he had understood the nature of addiction better, he would not have felt so ashamed to begin with, and he would have had less need to project a sense of blame on her. If Danielle had understood how addiction works, she would have been less prone to accept this blame.

Beyond taking responsibility for Scott's gambling, Danielle also blamed herself for the kind of person she had become. How could someone so goodhearted become so profoundly enraged?

We know that addiction is driven by rage, specifically rage at overwhelming helplessness. When Scott gambled he expressed that rage in the displaced action of his addiction. His need to perform his addiction was a purely internal matter. But of course it didn't have purely internal effects, and Danielle felt the full force of the rage behind Scott's addiction through its multiple destructive effects on her life. Indeed, the force of the rage behind Scott's gambling also made it hopeless for Danielle to do anything about his addictive behavior. The longer her efforts continued to be fruitless the more frustrating, and enraging, the situation was for her. As much as she tried every which way to deal with Scott and his addiction, she was powerless to do anything about it. In the end, although Scott had been dealing with an internal trap, it was now Danielle who was trapped. Like every other person when faced with utter powerlessness, she had a normal rage response.

When your partner suffers with addiction and you are powerless to help, it can easily make you feel trapped. The rage you may feel is a normal reaction under these circumstances, and is not due to any fundamental change in your character.

Danielle's personality had not changed any more than those people I described early in the book who find themselves trapped in a cave and start desperately screaming and pounding at the rocks.

How do you fix the relationship?

With a deeper understanding of the dynamics of addiction in relationships, Danielle and Scott could have avoided their escalation of blame and depression. Danielle needed to be clear in her own mind that she had no role in his gambling. That would help free her from guilt. Feeling less guilty, she would be less resentful of Scott and freed up to be more supportive. The cycle of anger between them would diminish.

It would likewise have been beneficial for Danielle to understand that her frustration and anger were unavoidable responses to Scott's behavior. Because Scott needed to protect his addiction by ignoring or defying anything Danielle did to "interfere" with it, Danielle was in a helpless, impossible position. Recognizing this would have allowed her to be far less critical of herself for being so angry. This, too, would have helped her to have more emotional energy to deal with the couple's problems.

For Scott's part, he would need to understand how enraging his behavior was to Danielle. It was hard for him to acknowledge that because of his shame. But Scott was also blind to how enraging his behavior was to Danielle because he believed she was reacting simply to the financial mess he had created. He didn't see that money problems were just one cause of Danielle's frustration. The other, actually larger frustration for her was the utter helplessness he was imposing on her by being unresponsive to anything she tried to do to intervene. In his focus on practical money issues, Scott was almost totally out of touch with Danielle's feelings. If he could have seen how trapped he made her feel he would have been more empathic. After all, his behavior may have been dominated by his need to repeat his addiction but, like Danielle, he was still the same person he had always been, and he still loved her. With greater appreciation of how frustrating his behavior was to her, the couple would have come closer together.

Of course, the eventual resolution of their problems would hinge on Scott mastering his addiction. For that, he would hopefully follow the steps outlined in this book, and if necessary, also seek professional help.

ADDICTIONS IN ADOLESCENTS

The question of how to deal with a family member with addiction is especially complicated when that member is an adolescent—usually a teenager, though some young people are still emotionally in adolescence into their early twenties. Here is a case that shows a common picture.

JANE

Jane's parents were at their wits' end when they had to deal with their eighteen-year-old daughter's disastrous behavior. Jane had left home and was living in another city, without a job, using drugs regularly. She called home when she needed money and for a while her parents sent it to her, since she told them (truthfully) that she would be homeless without the extra funds. But they knew perfectly well that she was using much, if not most, of that money to buy more drugs. As in the example I described earlier in this chapter, Jane's parents were urgently advised by friends and even some counselors that if they continued to send her money they were enabling her drug use. Someone even suggested to them that if Jane had an overdose of drugs and died, it would be basically their fault for supplying the money to obtain drugs.

What should they do? As always, a decision of this sort must be made thoughtfully, based on the individual situation. It is a mistake to try to follow any universal rule such as a supposed need to be tough or to not enable. The goal is to do what will be most helpful to the adolescent as well as to her parents. Fortunately, what is best for the adolescent is usually also best for the parents, for the simple reason that they love their child. This part of decision making, then, is just the same as with adults.

What does set adolescents apart, however, is that they are still growing. As everyone knows, growth in adolescence is regularly accompanied by turmoil and distress for both the adolescent and those around her. When your child is having trouble during this critical and difficult time, the first priority has to be ensuring that she survives to adulthood, when hopefully she will have better judgment and stability. This factor tilts decisions about dealing with the child, and with his or her addictions, toward providing more support—both financial and through parental guidance— than might be the case for a fully grown adult.

Jane lived in another city, and her parents' access to her was limited since she was intentionally unavailable except when she needed help. Under these circumstances, a reasonable approach for her parents would be to tell Jane that they would provide enough financial support to keep her off the street, but that they would send the funds directly to her landlord—and Jane would have to divulge her address. Food money and a small amount for living expenses would be sent directly to her, but in order to have this money she would have to be in treatment with someone in her city, the cost for which would be paid directly to the caregiver.

This solution is not foolproof, needless to say. Jane could still divert money to drugs, fail to attend treatment, and continue to create crises in which her parents would be called to provide emergency help. Should they provide it? Yes, for the reasons I offered above. It is better to be manipulated, lied to, or used than to have your child die or be seriously injured. In making these decisions it is important to remember, too, that people like Jane are generally skilled at finding drugs. If she did not have money to purchase them and was living on the street, she would still be likely, or even more likely, to find drugs through other means and suffer the consequences. Since enabling or not enabling people does not alter their addictive drive, it is unreasonable to assume that by withholding support from your child you can improve his or her addiction. So, as hard as it may be, the best thing you can do is to set what requirements you can, especially linking receipt of help to entering and staying in treatment, and look forward to the day when she or he is no longer an adolescent.

One more important point: once your child shows signs of significant distress, as in Jane's example, it is important to seek a good overall psychiatric evaluation. If her addiction is associated with a major mental disorder, you (and she) will need to know that, since treating this disorder will become a priority. The evaluation can also provide needed information about the child's risk of intentionally harming herself.

THE EFFECT OF A PARENT'S ADDICTION ON CHILDREN

As everyone knows, children's capacity to understand what is happening in their environment changes as they grow. This is also true of their ability to define and understand their own feelings. The emotional effect of a family member's addiction on a young child will depend therefore on both the child's age and the practical ways the child's life is impacted by the addiction.

Addictions are not always visible to a young child. For example, when a parent's addiction is compulsive gambling, there may be no addictive behavior visible to the child, only its consequences in the tension between the parents. Here, the concerns for the child are the same as in any family in which parents are fighting, angry, anxious, or depressed. In all such cases the ideal is for the parents (preferably both of them, either together or separately) to talk with the child to explain the tension in the family in language the child can grasp, and to reassure the child that he is safe and loved and will be forever.

Even more important than what is conveyed, however, is to listen to the child to learn what his concerns are. For a younger child, these may be unexpected, not realistically related to the actual problem facing the parents, and vastly different from what parents expect. Older children, on the other hand, may understand quite well what it means to lose money, for example, and why there is tension between the parents. That child is faced with dealing with what it means for a parent to have an addiction. It is this situation that is specific to addictions and that I will concentrate on below.

What Do Addictions Mean to a Child?

Depending on the age of the child, addiction in a parent may mean anything from a fundamental loss of safety to the loss of the child's sense of his or her own value.

The meaning of addiction to very young children

When addiction is visible to a very young child, as when a parent is drunk or high at home, it can be a very frightening experience. Children need to have—and assume that their parents are—powerful figures who are able to protect them. Parents are seen as capable of controlling the very young child's world. This sometimes leads to disappointment in parents when adverse events occur: a party that is rained out is cause to feel cheated by Mom and Dad, who should have controlled the weather ("But you promised!"). It is likewise taken for granted that parents can control themselves. They are omnipotent beings and need to be, to keep the child safe.

In this context, a parent who is clearly out of control of himself is a blow to a child's normal sense of safety. It is not Mommy or Daddy who is out of control; it is the world. Therefore, it is important that parents appreciate the extent of the fear such out-of-control behavior can create in their child. In talking with the child it is necessary to reassure him or her that both parents are still in control of the child's world. This may be far more important than, for instance, apologizing to the young child, or explaining the basis for the parent's behavior. The effects on very young children also underscore the importance of keeping out-of-control behavior out of their sight as much as possible.

The meaning of addiction to older children and adolescents

As a child grows, a parent's addiction shifts from producing global fear of a chaotic world to producing attempts to decipher the meaning of a parent's problem. An older child is also able to recognize a broader spectrum of addictive behavior. Gambling, binge eating, and other compulsive or addictive behaviors may now also be seen as indicators of a parent's loss of control.

The effects of a parent's addiction on an older child depend on the child's relationship with his parent, and the parents' ability to keep up healthy two-way communication with their child, allowing them to hear the child's thoughts and feelings so he does not have to be alone with his worries (which may be distorted and inflated compared to the real possibilities).

THE EFFECTS OF A PARENT'S ADDICTION ON A CHILD'S RESPECT AND SELF-RESPECT

All children, for their sense of safety and emotional well-being, need to be able to respect their parents. Parents who are respected enable children to feel safe because they believe their parents can be relied upon. And since children identify with their parents, seeing them in a positive light enables children to feel valuable themselves. This is especially true when children are younger, but continues through adolescence, although in the teenage years the importance of identification with parents is often masked by the normal rebelliousness of that age. Adolescents who say that they couldn't care less about what their parents are like are saying this because they are in the process of defining their own identities apart from their parents. But as long as they are not yet fully grown, that claim cannot be taken at face value, and the way parents behave is still important to their sense of themselves.

When parents behave erratically, as in addiction, they often lose the respect of their children, who experience a corresponding loss of safety and self-esteem. We, as adults with understanding of the nature of addiction, don't lose our respect for people suffering with addictions. But young people are not in that position. They have all the misperceptions about addiction that adults have had through the ages: that it is a sign of weakness, immorality, selfishness, and lack of caring or concern for others. These feelings may be expressed openly or kept secret. Older children and adolescents will often express themselves openly. With younger or less verbal children, the same feelings are likely present, however, so with them it takes a special attentiveness and ongoing acceptance of their feelings to help them express what they are secretly thinking. Either way, the task is to explain the nature of addiction in terms accessible to the child, with the goal of helping the child understand addiction as a sign of upset feelings in the parent who has addiction, and as a condition that has nothing to do with morality, weakness, or their love for their child.

It is also critical to let the child know that his anger, disappointment, and sadness are perfectly normal and completely justified. A child may have trouble with the duality of understanding both that the parent is suffering with a problem and that the child has every right to have her feelings, especially her anger. Even adults can have trouble with this, as we've discussed. People often think in terms of right and wrong, good and bad, making it hard to understand and value the feelings of both parties in a conflictual relationship. When it comes to children and their parents this is especially hard. Children want their parents to be good, wise, and strong. If they view their parents as lacking in these qualities it can throw them into turmoil. As a solution, to preserve that needed sense of a parent's goodness, children may instead blame themselves for problems. This may take the form of literally blaming themselves for the parent's behavior: "If only I hadn't made Daddy so upset he wouldn't have gotten drunk." Or, more insidiously, children may blame themselves for their angry feelings: "I must be a bad person to think such mad thoughts about Mommy." Either way, it is important to listen for these feelings in your child and to reassure him about them. A mother might say to her son, "If my mother did what I did, I'd be angry with her too. Actually, I am angry with me. We're both upset about what I did. Let's be sure we keep talking about how we both feel about me when I do things like that."

The Effects of a Parent's Addiction on a Child's Trust

Trusting parents overlaps with respecting them, of course. Just like adults, children lose respect for untrustworthy people, including their parents. There is also another issue with untrustworthiness. Once parents are deemed untrustworthy they are less likely to be approached for help or guidance. In the case of addictions, this means children may be less willing or able to listen to your explanations of the problem.

Younger children in particular may take your untrustworthiness in one instance—such as saying you won't repeat an addictive behavior—as evidence that you are untrustworthy in general. Consequently, it is wise to adhere to the following rule:

Never tell a child (or adolescent or adult for that matter)
that an addictive behavior—on your part or the part
of your spouse—will never happen again. That sort
of promise, even though it is tempting to make in
the moment in order to help the child feel better, is a
disappointment waiting to happen.

But even saying that you will try your hardest to stop is easily heard as a promise by children. After all, you are a powerful
figure to a young child and if you say you'll try your hardest, she
will assume that you will succeed. So, when talking to your child
it is better to describe how difficult it is for you (or your spouse)
to manage the feelings that lead to addictive behavior. You can
certainly add that you or your spouse is trying to control it, but
to avoid disappointing her or losing her trust, you should go out
of your way to explain that the behavior is likely to continue for
a while, at least. If the behavior then does not diminish, it will be
important to be open with your child about that, too. This will
help lessen feelings that he or she has been lied to, and help the
child express his or her own feelings of frustration and sadness.

Trust is best maintained not by promising to change
addictive behavior but by being honest about how hard it is
to manage, and by demonstrating trustworthiness in other
areas, outside the context of the addiction.

Older children and adolescents are less likely to globalize a
lack of trust and more likely to see the problem as separate from
other areas of the parent's trustworthiness. For them, the bigger

problem may be that they can't turn to the parent with addiction for advice. This might be expressed as, "Why should I ask you about how to do anything, you can't even control your own life!" Certainly, this involves loss of respect for the parent whose overall value is seen as tarnished, but there is a more specific sense that views about life from this parent cannot be trusted. Since children and adolescents regularly need help in making decisions, this is a real loss for them. Young people regularly turn to each other for advice and information about difficult decisions—sometimes with bad results—and they are likely to do this even more if they feel their parents are not trustworthy guides.

As with younger children, honesty and openness are crucial in maintaining, or rebuilding, your child's trust. As they grow older, children idealize their parents less, and can better appreciate hearing of the struggle with addiction that parents are going through. It is helpful to adopt an open attitude that says, "I'm having an awful time trying to control this addiction, and I know it's hard on you and the family. But I'm still your father/mother. I've still lived a lot of life, and I'm not dumb. I can still give you some good advice about things or help you to think about your problems. Just don't ask me when I'm upset/drunk/bingeing. And I'll try not to give you advice when I'm in that state, either!"

SPECIAL CONSIDERATIONS WHEN DISCUSSING ADDICTION WITH YOUNG CHILDREN

When discussing addiction with your child, and listening to your child's concerns, keep in mind that his fears and anxieties may be distorted and extreme compared to your own way of thinking. For example, when a small child's father is drunk, or secluded in a room watching a sports event on which he has a bet, the child may tell you that his father hates him—or even wants to kill him. Perhaps you're prepared for the child's notion that his father is angry with him, but his fear of being murdered may well come as a surprise. Yet, such thoughts are commonplace in young children, for whom primal feelings are close to the surface. In other cases, a child might interpret a parent's behavior as suicidal, or express thoughts about harming the parent or parts of the parent's body. Or children may include the entire world in their thinking. The world will end, or monsters will eat the house, the child, or a parent. Mostly, as you can see, these thoughts suggest the fear and aggression with which the child is living. But they also may have a distinctly depressive quality. Fearing the end of the world can suggest a child's sense of some imminent catastrophe, but it can also refer to her loneliness and despair. It is important to try to hear whatever feelings your child is conveying in her own manner.

By talking with your child about her feelings and correcting your child's disproportionate fears, you reinforce her sense of security, and disconnect her feelings from the scary ideas she has invented. Here's an example:

> TIMMY (*a four-year-old who's just been tucked into bed*):
> Mommy, I'm afraid to go to sleep when Daddy is acting funny. I'm afraid he'll come in and hurt me.
> MOTHER: Daddy would never hurt you. He loves you. Why do you think that?

By adding this question, rather than only reassuring Timmy, his mother lets him know that his thoughts and feelings are okay to have and that she wants him to tell her about them.

> TIMMY: Daddy scares me when he gets like that.
> MOTHER: What scares you?
> TIMMY: He gets different. He gets crazy.
> MOTHER: What do you mean, "crazy"?

TIMMY: He's all crazy. It's like a monster, like the monster I saw on TV. He got crazy and killed people.

MOTHER: Daddy would never hurt you. He's not a monster.

TIMMY: But he acts like a monster.

MOTHER: Sometimes he gets upset, and that scares you. I know why he gets that way. He gets worried about things, then he drinks alcohol and that makes him feel worse. Daddy knows about this, too, and he's trying to get better at dealing with his upset feelings. He and I talk about it together, so it doesn't scare me. Maybe we can both talk with him about it, too, tomorrow, so you don't have to be so scared. Anyway, getting upset the way he does doesn't mean he's a monster! He's not green, you know!

TIMMY: I know, but he acts like that.

MOTHER: I know you get scared. It's hard to be scared. I used to be scared when I was a little girl and my mommy or daddy got upset.

TIMMY: You were?

MOTHER: Oh sure. I used to tell myself stories when I was scared, about being in beautiful places. What do you do when you're scared?

TIMMY: I don't know.

MOTHER: Well, what did you do when Daddy got upset last time?

TIMMY: I just hid in my bed.

MOTHER: Okay. You don't tell yourself stories?

TIMMY: No.

MOTHER: Well, maybe we can think about other ways you can feel better when you're scared.

TIMMY: I don't know.

MOTHER: Let's see if we can think of things.

TIMMY (*sitting up*): I could wear my Superman clothes.

MOTHER: That's a good idea. What else?

TIMMY (*energized now*): I could get a suit of armor, and a sword.

MOTHER: Okay. What else?

TIMMY: I could have a whole army (*waving his arms*). I'd say, "Come on, men, let's get 'em." (*He makes wild, stabbing motions.*)

MOTHER: Hold on! You're supposed to be going to sleep. Look, Daddy would never hurt you. He just gets upset sometimes, but I know all about it and so does he, and we're working hard on it. Let's talk more about this in the morning, okay? We can talk about some other things you can do when you get scared. And we can talk to Daddy, too. Okay?

TIMMY: Can I leave the light on?

MOTHER: Okay. Good night.

TIMMY: Good night.

Timmy still needed the light on, but his mother helped him by explaining his father's problem in a way Timmy could grasp and by helping Timmy focus on—and share with her—his scared feelings. She did not deny his fear or try to talk him out of it, and she did not deny the reality of his father's scary behavior. But she directed his attention toward his feelings rather than a real risk of being killed. Timmy didn't have to be alone with his fears because his mother knew about them, she had experienced them herself, and she was there to help with them. If he was able to talk with his father the next day, that would be best of all, to reassure him and to help him resume seeing his father as his ally, not his enemy.

With older children and adolescents, of course, the conversation will be more reality-oriented, in keeping with the child's greater understanding of the nature of the problem. But even with older children, it is a good idea to keep one ear open to thoughts you might assume your child would have outgrown long ago. After all, your child knows what is expected of him at his age, so these less grown-up concerns may be the most embarrassing thoughts to have, and make him the most lonely. If you are accepting of them it will be a big help.

————

In Part Four, the final section of this book, I'll discuss how treatment professionals can use the steps we've discussed to treat people with addictions. If you are not a therapist you should feel completely free to skip it without feeling you have missed something. By having read through to this point, you have already, I hope, come to see addiction as it really is—a common emotional symptom that can be mastered and controlled once its psychological nature is understood.

PART IV

For the Professional

The steps I have outlined for breaking addiction can also serve as a guide to treating someone with addiction. I call the approach based on the steps in this book AFT, for "addiction focused treatment." You may have already begun to think about how you could adapt the steps in the case stories to help a person (or a couple) seeking treatment with you. In this chapter, I'll discuss how to do that, as well as some related clinical issues.

THE BEGINNING:
STEP 1 AND STEP 2

People seek treatment at different points in their struggle with addiction. Step 1, which focused mainly on diagnosing addiction, may not be necessary for some people. But even people who are well aware that they are suffering from addiction may harbor the kinds of misconceptions about addiction that I described in Part One. These misconceptions, or myths, will need to be dispelled before you proceed with treatment. The so-called chronic

brain disease model of addiction, which has received much attention lately in the media, is a particularly common and distracting
myth that you may have to debunk before proceeding. Likewise,
the mistaken idea that addictions make a person different from
the rest of humanity, which I discussed in Step 2, is also usually necessary and helpful to reject even for those people who
know they have an addiction. Explaining how addictions are
symptoms, just like other compulsive behaviors, opens the door
to treating behaviors your patient[6] may not have considered to
be addictions. When a patient sees that these other compulsive
activities are simply different manifestations of the same drive to
reverse helplessness, you can both track the vicissitudes of your
patient's addictive behavior as it changes form. When your patient says she has stopped drinking but now cannot stop shopping
online, you will have laid the groundwork for her to recognize
this new behavior as another incarnation of her old addiction.
Though the original presenting symptom has disappeared, together you can make use of this new compulsive behavior as a
fresh opportunity to look at the precipitants behind these behaviors. Explaining the dynamics of addiction to people helps them
focus beyond the object of their addiction—drugs, food, shopping, or gambling—to the root of their problem. By not talking about alcohol, bingeing, or gambling, you save a great deal
of time—time that can be spent discussing overwhelming feelings of loss, anger, sadness, or shame. Likewise, it does patients a
great deal of good to see that what they seek is not a drink or a
bet, but a sense of empowerment in the face of old and persistent
feelings of helplessness.

---

[6] I am using the term "patient" in this chapter because it is the tradition in my field, but I
am aware that the word "client" is the tradition in other therapeutic fields. The terms are
interchangeable and I use "patient" here solely for convenience.

STEP 3

Step 3 brings us to the first major treatment focus: clarifying the nature of the key moment on the path to addiction. Attuning patients to the fact that the psychological mechanism of addiction is put in gear long before they actually engage in addictive behavior, entirely shifts their understanding of their addiction. This shift is crucial to everything that follows in treatment. It enables people to see what is about to happen in their lives, and to have time to understand the emotional factors producing their addiction. It allows time to think through alternative, more direct solutions before they are overwhelmed.

A therapist can be a big help in defining and identifying these key moments. From a technical standpoint, this may mean having to interrupt patients in the course of recounting their addictive episodes, if they pass right by the key moment and focus on the ill effects of their addictive behavior, instead. But focusing a great deal of time on the after-effects of addictive behavior is of limited value. Of course, you will want to hear about effects of an addiction when they have produced deeply important feelings, such as grief about bad decisions and lost opportunities that have resulted from the addiction. But it is unwise to dwell on these consequences of addictive acts since they tend to distract attention from the real work of the treatment, which is about the *causes* of addiction, not their effects.

STEP 4

The essential goal in Step 4 is to identify your patient's defensive style, which can blind him to the key moment in the path to his addictive act. Defenses and defensive style are not easily transformed, however, because they are part of a person's character—his or her ways of dealing with challenging, frightening, or painful feelings—which has developed over a lifetime. Since you are focusing on the addiction, however, it is enough at this point to help your patient see the ways she keeps herself from knowing the feelings and issues that precipitate addictive urges.

Because people are routinely unable to see their own defenses, a therapist may be especially helpful here. And since people use the same defenses and defensive style in the rest of their lives as they do with their addictions, there will be many opportunities to show these mechanisms at work in other areas of a person's life. Seeing the same defenses everywhere, such as intellectualization and obsessionalism to avoid feelings, becoming vague and confused to keep from knowing things that are upsetting, projecting one's thoughts and feelings to the outside world so they don't have to be owned as one's own thoughts, or simply being action-oriented in place of bearing unpleasant feelings, will help people recognize these defenses when they occur on the path toward addictive behavior.

Recognizing the emotional mechanisms they use in their lives can also help people appreciate how their addictions, too, are no more or less than psychological symptoms to deal with feelings. Just as they can come to understand other ways they deal with their emotions, so they can understand their addictions. Seeing this can mean less unnecessary discouragement or hopelessness about both their addictions and themselves.

STEP 5

Having located the key moment in Step 3, in Step 5 the focus turns to the feelings of helplessness that precipitate the key moment.

Becoming attuned to feelings of helplessness is actually a skill people can develop with experience and with a therapist's help. As you highlight the circumstances in your patient's life that give rise to overwhelming feelings of helplessness, she will develop the ability to anticipate these occasions for herself. Indeed, she will learn that these moments of feeling trapped are actually rather common. Knowing the connection between these trapped moments and the addictive acts that follow them means she will be able to predict "high-risk" situations—circumstances in the future that are particularly likely to provoke feelings of helplessness, and thus spark her addictive drive. Because this skill is so clearly useful, patients regularly become quite good at identifying the kinds of experiences that will provoke feelings of helplessness, and their addictive acts.

Recognizing the circumstances that provoke feelings of helplessness is also critical because it is like a Broadway-sized neon arrow pointing directly at a person's central emotional issues. As we know, the factors that lead a person to feel overwhelmingly helpless are always the same as those that lead to his or her emotional problems in life in general. In the many cases we've examined throughout this book we've seen examples of underlying issues that produce the compulsion to repeat an addictive behavior. By helping to identify the specific emotional factors in your patient that make him feel overwhelmingly helpless, you will be in position to explore and treat these deeper issues, reducing the sense of helplessness and the need for an addictive response.

A question of timing, however, remains: how far should you go in exploring these underlying issues now, versus at a later point in treatment? I will return to this question later in this chapter. For the moment, though, the major point is this:

Since addiction is part of a person's overall psychology—a symptom produced by the same issues that trouble a person in general—it is always useful to integrate treatment of addiction with a broader view of your patient's psychological landscape. Understanding addiction helps to understand all other areas of trouble, and understanding other areas of trouble in a person's life helps to understand the addiction.

STEP 6

Step 6 focuses on finding more direct ways to reverse feelings of helplessness in place of an addictive act. This process is more or less the same in treatment as it is for a person dealing with his addiction by himself. However, once you and your patient have established the nature and cause of his helplessness trap, you can together consider partial, good-enough solutions to alleviate his sense of being cornered and powerless. These solutions may seem obvious and would usually be clear to your patient, too, if he were a third-person observer. Here's where a therapist's point of view is valuable; by pointing to the functions that the addiction is serving, you enable him to see for himself the practical alternatives to his addictive behavior—actions he can take that address his underlying dilemma more directly than the addiction. As people develop experience noticing not just the key moments along the route to the final behavior but also the alternative pathways open to them, they can become adept at catching themselves well before they repeat their addictive behavior.

A therapist can also be especially helpful in the situations in which there's no simple, direct action that can reverse the helplessness trap, as when there is the loss of a loved one. Here, the therapist's job is to help the patient refocus his attention from the loss itself to what the loss *means* to him. In Step 6 I described Gil, whose imminent breakup with his girlfriend led to powerful urges to use heroin. The breakup was a traumatic event for Gil because it evoked earlier deeply painful losses and the meaning to Gil of those losses. But Gil had focused strictly on the actual loss of his girlfriend. Treatment would be focused on helping him see that it was an old belief in the inevitability of being abandoned that had been resurrected by his current loss. Further, it was this resurrected idea that was the deeper source of his overwhelming hopelessness and helplessness, and consequently the basis for his urge to use heroin. This shift in perspective—facilitated by therapy—transforms Gil's helplessness trap into a potentially understandable and workable problem.

Of course, these sorts of transformations can take time, and require a capacity for self-observation that takes real work to develop. Many people are not used to inspecting the roots of their most profound anxieties and fears. In Step 6, I compared the capacity for such self-observation to the ability to float ten feet above your head, looking down on yourself to consider more thoughtfully what might be making you as upset as you are. Developing this capacity can be difficult, but it is necessary to understand and master one's emotional life and behavior, in general. Working with patients to understand the way they experience the events that trigger addictive thoughts is, then, a prime opportunity not only for treating addiction; it is also important work on behalf of a person's overall emotional health.

STEP 7

Since the final step involves recognizing and working with the underlying issues that lead to addiction, and have been present throughout a person's life, it is perhaps the step that most benefits from a therapist's help. Certainly people can do some of this work on their own, as I've described throughout this book. But because many of the feelings, thoughts, and confusions that buttress and perpetuate addiction are never completely in one's awareness, nobody can do all of this work him- or herself. It takes a second, professional perspective to fully bring what is not conscious or what is carefully guarded out into the open. As I've said above, exploring these deeper issues establishes the basis for expanding the focus of your work even after the addiction is resolved, to treat the entire person. This is a good thing in itself, and helps guarantee that when further challenges arise in your patient's life, he will be prepared for them without having to return to his addictive solution.

TIMING

Since addictions are emotional symptoms embedded in the substance of a patient's larger emotional life, exploring and understanding them always overlaps with exploring and understanding other areas of emotional life. And it should be clear that exploring areas not directly connected with addictions is absolutely necessary to fully understand the narrower concerns that produce the addiction symptom. However, there is still a question of how much and when to allow or encourage the treatment to branch out to consider these other areas.

This question is more relevant in the treatment of addictions than in the treatment of other problems—even of other compulsions that are psychologically identical. The risks posed by many addictive behaviors may necessitate a narrower focus on this behavior, at least until it is not an immediate danger to your patient or those around him or her. In practice, this means keeping track of your patient's addictive behavior more closely than you would if it were not dangerous. It is usually not useful, for instance, to track the details of a person's hand-washing or need to ritually plump up pillows before going to sleep, even though these compulsive behaviors may be psychologically identical to compulsive drug use. But with hazardous behaviors it is more important to stay aware of them at least enough to make decisions about such things as the need for hospitalization or medical intervention. On the other hand, once you are confident of what ongoing level of risk is involved, there is no therapeutic value in keeping track of day-to-day fluctuations in addictive behaviors. A patient may, for instance, drink four or five glasses of wine every night for a year—while he is in treatment. Nothing is gained by asking about this every time you see him. This is different, of course, from paying close attention to times when your patient reports that his addictive urges have sharply increased, or they recur after a period of abstinence. It is just these occasions when a great deal can be learned about the factors and issues that produce the person's addictive drive.

Attending to potentially harmful behavior is a priority ahead of other longer-term concerns. In most cases, though, emergencies are infrequent. If there is no crisis, then it is both appropriate and helpful to spend a good deal of time and effort exploring, branching out, to learn as much as possible about all factors in your patient's emotional life.

SHOULD TREATMENT FOR ADDICTION BE SEPARATE FROM THE REST OF A PERSON'S PSYCHOTHERAPY?

It is unfortunately a common misconception among therapists, even today, that treatment for addiction should be pursued separately from a patient's overall therapy. Separating addiction from other treatment makes as little sense as taking any other symptom—say, a fear of closeness—and sending a patient elsewhere to address that issue while you try to understand and treat his depressed mood. Since addictions are emotional symptoms, they should be treated together with everything else troubling a person, because they are always related to everything else. Understanding what makes a patient depressed will help him understand why he has developed an addiction, and understanding his addiction will help explain why he is depressed. Why, then, do people so often divide addiction from general psychological treatment?

Part of the reason is historical. For many years therapists had no idea about the psychological nature of addiction, and therefore could offer little help. It made some sense to send people away to others who said they could treat the problem. Indeed, it was probably a relief to those therapists to have somewhere to send these folks. But if you are a therapist able to understand how addiction works, you do not need to send your patients away. In fact, when therapists do send their patients away for the "addiction part" of their treatment, they are doing something quite destructive. They are telling patients that they, the therapists, are either not competent or not interested in treating this problem. Either message is harmful, suggesting that either the addiction or the person is so different from other people that she or he cannot be understood by you.

Further, if examination of a person's addiction is removed from his treatment, the treatment can obviously never be complete. It would be like saying to someone, "I will treat your anxiety, but talk to the fellow down the hall about your depression." People simply cannot be chopped up like that, and neither can their treatment. In the event that you are in the midst of treating a patient with addiction and feel you are in over your head, the best course of action is to seek consultation with another therapist with more experience with the ideas I've described in this book. You will then have the advantage of that person's knowledge without disrupting what may be a very useful and meaningful therapy between you and your patient.

HOSPITALIZATION

Sometimes it may be necessary to interrupt therapy because a patient requires hospitalization. Usually this is because an addictive behavior has become so hazardous that a break is needed, in a safe place. It is beyond the focus of this book to discuss hospitalization options. However, if hospitalization is needed, any interruption in a patient's therapy should be minimized as much as possible. You will be the person caring for your patient long after his hospitalization; your work with your patient will be the backbone of his treatment. Therefore, it is ideal if you can continue to meet or speak with your patient on the phone during hospitalization. At the least you will want to be in touch with the inpatient caregivers throughout your patient's stay in a facility.

Following discharge, many patients feel energized and encouraged. This is good. But it is your job to bear in mind that no inpatient stay, regardless of how well designed and managed, can cure the problem. Consequently, no matter how motivated your patient feels after leaving the hospital, it is important that you continue to steadily point out the factors that are still present in the person's mind and that can lead to future addictive behavior. Relapses very frequently occur after a hospitalization—sometimes almost immediately after discharge—so while enjoying a patient's good feelings after his time away, it is best that you and your patient together anticipate the almost inevitable future problems.

IMPATIENCE IN TREATING ADDICTION

Though the pessimistic attitude many therapists have toward addiction treatment is undeserved, there is no question that it can be challenging work. One reason for this is that addictions so often are injurious behaviors. This produces extra tension and extra pressure on caregivers to do something quickly to make the behaviors stop. Sometimes this pressure arises from the patient himself, who is understandably impatient to be rid of such a destructive problem. Just as often, pressure comes from family members who have suffered the consequences of a person's addictive behavior and are both angry and worried. If you, as the therapist, cannot "fix" the problem quickly—if your patient continues to drink or gamble, etc., for months or even years—you may well become the target of all that anger and frustration.

Being blamed for not stopping addictive behavior is a hazard of this work. When people suffer with other, perhaps equally serious, problems of depression or anxiety, therapists are routinely given the time and space to do their work. There is an implicit understanding by both patients and their families that lifelong problems require a long time to work out. When people with these problems are finished with their treatment, perhaps years later, they and their loved ones are delighted to see how far they have come and how happy and fulfilled they are now.

Those treating addictions may not be viewed so patiently. More than one therapist has heard protests such as, "What kind of treatment is this? My husband is still drinking and you've been seeing him for a whole year!" In responding to this criticism it is useful to remember that those protesting are doing so mostly because they do not understand the nature of addiction. If they see addiction as a bad habit, or something that can be cured through so-called tough love, they will naturally be angry and disappointed that the treatment takes so long. In these situations, explaining how addiction works as I have done in this book is sometimes helpful. (Suggesting that family members obtain a copy of the book for themselves may also be helpful.) But of course, family members are not your patients and they may not be willing or interested to hear about why their loved one is still doing his behavior. And they did not sign up to learn something from you about themselves. They just want the addiction to stop. Accordingly, they need to know that you have heard them, and that you are both aware of the risks to your patient and as concerned about these risks as they are. It often helps family members to bear their anxiety when they see that while treatment takes time, it is not because you are treating the problem casually, or are underestimating its severity. You are in it together with your patient and with them.

In the end, the best antidote to your feeling overwhelmed by the attacks of others is to know both the nature of addiction and your patient. The more you understand the person you are trying to help and his or her addiction, the more you will be able to tolerate accusations that you are not fixing him or her fast enough.

Fortunately, the difficulties in treating addictions are outweighed by the fact that they are very treatable when approached correctly. The ultimate reward for your and your patients' hard work is seeing your patients' lives turned around.

ACKNOWLEDGMENTS

This book was made possible by the warm and generous response to my first book, *The Heart of Addiction*. To all of those who were open to trying a new and very different approach to treating addiction I give my sincere thanks.

My wife, Connie, a gifted writer, read every word of this book before anyone else, and when the work pleased her keen eye I knew it was ready to be seen by others. She also put up with my requests to have her read and reread sections I toiled over. She sustained my work on this book as she has my life.

I give thanks also to my editor at HarperCollins, Jason Sack. Besides being a pleasure to work with, he offered many valuable suggestions that have much improved the book's readability.

I received help with everything from thinking up descriptive words to ideas for cover design from Zachary Dodes, Joshua Dodes, Farrah Dodes, Pamela Douglas, and Rowena Raborar — there's nothing better than family, and I thank them all.

Zick Rubin helped me find my terrific agent, Ed Walters, and I am grateful to both of them.

Last but of course not least, I must repeat what I said in my first book: that my work in addiction would not have been possible without the many patients who have allowed me to know about their lives, both inner and outer, and to share with me their journey toward understanding themselves. My great thanks to each of them.

INDEX

BOOKS BY LANCE DODES

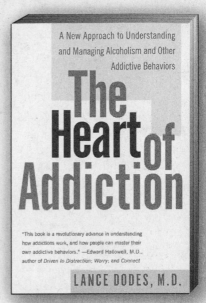

BREAKING ADDICTION
A 7-Step Handbook for Ending Any Addiction

ISBN 978-0-06-198739-7 (paperback)

"Dr. Dodes looks beneath the surface behaviors of addiction to root them out at their source. . . . This groundbreaking work should become the 'go to' handbook for anyone suffering with addiction. . . . I highly recommend it."
—*Edward M. Hallowell, M.D.,* author of *Answers to Distraction*

THE HEART OF ADDICTION
A New Approach to Understanding and Managing Alcoholism and Other Addictive Behaviors

ISBN 978-0-06-095803-9 (paperback)

"Dodes makes a cogent case for a new way of looking at addictions. Rejecting many commonly held and rarely questioned beliefs . . . Dodes offers an original voice to the recovery field and a fresh look at a formidable problem for individuals, families and society."
—*Publishers Weekly*